EVERY PASTOR NEEDS A PASTOR

EVERY PASTOR NEEDS A PASTOR

Louis McBurney

WORD BOOKS
PUBLISHER
WACO, TEXAS

To my parents

ROBERT AND LOUISE MCBURNEY

for giving me faith in God,
in others, and in myself.

Acknowledgments

I gratefully thank

. . . Fred Smith and Floyd Thatcher who first suggested I write this book.

. . . My teachers who helped prepare me.

. . . My friends who trusted our relationship enough to criticize my efforts, especially Jim Denton, Greg Livingston, and Don Anderson.

. . . My Board of Directors at Marble Retreat: Scott Middleton, Ed Bratcher, and Byrn Williamson, Jr. They have encouraged and selflessly supported this dream as well as working through early manuscripts.

. . . My secretaries, Nancy Neal, Joan Spicer, and Patti Taylor, who persisted so patiently and cheerfully.

. . . My patients who have courageously shared their hurts.

. . . And my family: Melissa, Bruce, Andrea, and Brent, who love me.

Contents

8 Contents

Foreword

The last ten years have seen an explosion of concern over interpersonal relationships. In business, government, schools, and churches, groups have formed to help people learn to know themselves and each other. We have identified the forces which have increased isolation, such as increased mobility, the breakdown of the extended family, the population explosion, pollution, lawlessness, television, etc. Significant gains have been made toward restoring a sense of community. We are more aware of the emotional needs of those around us. This developing of caring groups represents one of the most loving acts of man to have occurred in recent history.

In the midst of the T-groups, love-ins, awareness seminars, and enrichment conferences, however, there often stands one man apart. He may even be "leading" the group. He is sought out by the desperate, the lonely, the misunderstood, the alcoholic—all the hurting, forgotten elements of society. He consoles, encourages, counsels, supports, and loves. A sensitive, concerned, and committed person, he is often alone, sometimes hurt and frightened, but strangely ignored. He is the local minister.

Introduction

When spring finally breaks softly through the snow of a Minnesota winter, there is a real cause for celebration. Six months of ice and bone-chilling wind is quite enough, and daffodils are a welcome sight.

One delightfully warm and fragrant spring evening our light-heartedness was suddenly interrupted. A new acquaintance, a minister's wife from a nearby community, was at our door anxiously asking to talk. Her eyes were red from crying. Her voice was strained and her hands nervously twisted a tear-soaked handkerchief. For the next two hours she sobbed out her story: marital problems, difficulty within the church, and a deepening depression in her husband. I had known him for some time through his hospital work as a chaplain trainee, and in recent months I had sensed his despondency. Although I had tried to open the door for him to unburden, he never could do so. She continued to see me from time to time, but he remained defensive and frightened, refusing to be counseled. The last I heard they had separated, and he had resigned from the ministry. In the months that followed I became aware of the despair and pain endured by this man and by several other ministers.

Not long after that first sad encounter with our friend, I was called to give a psychiatric opinion in one of our hospitals. A minister's wife had been admitted for evaluation of chest pains. No organic disease had been found. My interview with her revealed several areas of psychological conflict, ranging from resentment toward the church to a feeling of sexual unfulfillment related to her husband's disinterest. Most of my patients with similar problems eagerly, though fearfully, accept psychotherapy. This tearful, hurting, defeated woman would not.

"What would the church members say if they ever found out?" she responded, and she returned home still carrying her heartache.

Next came an anxiety-ridden nun who had struggled with abrupt changes in her secure and ordered world. After years of being set apart from close personal relationships, and serving her community in a highly structured environment, she was suddenly expected to accept freedom from rules and express her individuality. Both concepts terrified her.

Then there came an evangelist who inexplicably lost his voice whenever he faced a congregation. Feelings of anger and resentment deep within his unconscious were finding expression in this sudden, highly significant way. His previously unspoken desire to quit preaching had found an acceptable outlet. Now he would neither have to verbalize his anger, nor would he be seen as a "quitter," options too threatening for him to choose.

A foreign missionary, home on medical leave, sought help for his growing obsessive-compulsive behavior. He had become obsessed by sexual fantasies. These caused him great pain and guilt, and he was immobilized by compulsive rituals. Always a clean and orderly individual, now he could not escape from a need to reorder, organize, and sterilize his environment and his thoughts.

These incidents began to draw my attention to the peculiar problems borne by the clergy today. At a time when my own spiritual pilgrimage was marked by joy and renewal, I sadly learned that thousands of disillusioned clergymen leave the pastorate every year, frequently because of emotional problems. I began to ask questions regarding religious vocational life. How is a man called into the ministry? What expectations does he have, and what are the demands placed on him by the church? What are his problems and their psychological roots? Why is it so difficult for him to seek help? What are the effects of the ministry on his wife and family?

On the following pages, I want to share some of my impressions with you. They come out of twenty-five years as a Christian deeply involved in the church, and seven years as a psychiatrist probing for answers. I've also included some applicable guidelines to mental health and emotional survival for the man of God.

Part I

The Call:

Invited or Inducted?

Jesus was walking by the Sea of Galilee when he saw two brothers, Simon called Peter and his brother Andrew, casting a net into the lake; for they were fishermen. Jesus said to them, "Come with me and I will make you fishers of men." And at once they left their nets and followed him (Matt. 4:18–20 NEB).

One bright, warm Sunday morning in April, 1952, I strode eagerly toward Sunday school as usual. Our class was a rowdy gang of fourteen-year-olds, but our teacher, an indestructible college freshman, had brought us to a joyous commitment to Christ. He was also pretty adept at dodging paper airplanes.

After Bible study we giggled and poked our way down to the first three rows on the left side of the sanctuary, our unchallenged territory. There we gathered week after week to sing loudly, snicker, squirm, write notes, and more recently, to notice how different the girls were looking.

I remember little of the worship service that momentous Sunday, and absolutely nothing of Dr. Metcalf's message, but I will never forget the last fifteen minutes of that hour. Oblivious to the notes and whispers, I experienced a strange heaviness in my chest and a lump in my throat. As I struggled uncomfortably in my seat, I don't remember hearing any voices, but I was overpowered by the conviction that God wanted my life. When the invitation hymn, "Where He Leads Me I Will Follow," was sung, and the altar call was given, I bolted tearfully forward the five paces to the front and choked out my decision. I had "surrendered to special service."

It should not be surprising that an adolescent makes this life-changing decision. Just emerging from the limited perspectives of a narrowly confined childhood existence, he is developing awareness of himself as a maturing individual. The great issues of life are beginning to enter his consciousness.

Eric Erickson characterizes this stage of development as confronting the issue of "identification" versus "isolation." This applies not only to one's identification with a peer group but to the broader community of man. Coupled with the idealism and enthusiasm of youth, many adolescents experience, as I did, an urgent need to commit their energies to improving the quality of life for mankind. The ultimate manifestation of this humanitarian urge will be determined by a multiplicity of factors. These are different for each individual: physical abilities, intellect, interests, parents' expectations and value system, birth order, socioeconomic level, the needs and desires of the community, and religious experience.

Now let's consider aspects of "the call."

1

Called: to What?

At the age of fourteen I initially felt that my "call" was to become a preacher. I might easily have become locked into this slot and been influenced to suppress any doubt or dissatisfaction with that choice. But fortunately that didn't happen. The openness and flexibility of those around me allowed me to explore ways of acting on my commitment, so I was equally comfortable pursuing drama with the thought of applying those skills to serving God. A later decision to study medicine carried little anxiety and no guilt, and I later felt equal freedom to choose psychiatry as a medical specialty. My basic commitment has never waned and the directional changes have occurred only after thought and prayer. A young person should have this same freedom to switch from science to theology, or from industry to agriculture, as he answers God's unique call in his life.

Freedom Is Important

The importance of allowing freedom for an individual to find his own call cannot be overemphasized. All too frequently the choices are forced, or at least strongly impressed upon the person. Within many denominations, unfortunately, the only way to serve God has been perceived as being through the ordained ministry. The most regrettable aspect of this opinion has been the unhappiness of those who were ill-equipped by ability or motivation to fill the role of clergyman. We desperately need to educate our church members in this area and avoid pushing talented Christians willy-nilly into pulpits while business, science, agriculture, sports, education, industry, government, and the entertainment world cry out for Christian witness. Fortunately, my community and my parents had learned that lesson.

By contrast, a college professor I know reported a far different experience. He felt a call similar to mine. His stimulating speaking ability, his winsome personality, and his religious community established his vocational choice as the pastoral ministry. He enjoyed early affirmation of this as a youth evangelist, but when doubts arose and conflicts developed, he felt trapped and unable to look for alternatives. Like many others, he had sensed from his environment the unspoken conditions of approval: "We adore and cherish you as a preacher, but don't expect our acceptance of you in any other role. You *have been called—to preach!* Any other use of your talents will be a denial of God and of us who have taught you and helped you find your call." There was even the added pressure of having received financial help in college and seminary in order to meet that call.

It is understandable that under such circumstances he felt too obligated to his community to seriously consider a change. They might not understand—in fact, they probably would not. Years later, after completing seminary training, he felt compelled to pursue a doctoral program in another field, ultimately accepting an appointment as a professor of economics.

A tragic result of his experience was a deep-seated resentment toward the system which "inducted" him into the ministry by interpreting his call for him. He bitterly dismissed the whole business as a dreadful mistake, no, worse than a mistake, a sneaky trick pulled off against him by a provincial community. In his attempt to escape he threw out as much of his cultural foundation as possible, leaving himself denuded and isolated. He now says wistfully, "I wish I had some faith. Maybe I tossed out the baby with the bath water." Was his call invalid, or was it simply misunderstood and misinterpreted?

Common Problem

His resentment is not uncommon. I hear many ministers ask, "How could God do this to me? I have been used, abused, and miserable because as an enthusiastic young man I made an impulsive decision." One ex-pastor put it this way: "I'm tired of God calling me collect all the time. Every time he talks with me, I'm the one who has to pay for it."

The problem seems to be in differentiating between what "God has done to us" and what we do to ourselves. We not only hear and accept God's call, but we also shoulder the burden of saving the institutions. Rather than invest ourselves in bearing the hurts of men, we are spent in an endless effort to support the organization. We occupy ourselves with trying to keep the organization afloat. We don't fish for men. We're too busy bailing out the boat.

Bailing out the boat can become unbearable. You may feel like Bryan, an enthusiastic, tireless young man called into Christian service. After seminary he applied all his strength and ingenuity to the program of his denomination and his pastorate. His work bore positive fruits, and he was rewarded by promotions to larger and more influential churches. With each promotion he found himself less involved with people, and more and more inundated by the tide of administrative matters.

When he finally came to the realization that he was spending more time "bailing" than "fishing," he had the courage and wisdom to interrupt the cycle. He resigned from his pastorate for a period of retreat to reevaluate "self" and "call," and reassign priorities. He has now reentered the pastoral ministry, but with a new concept of his gifts and how to use them.

For others this process of taking stock has led to ministry through counseling, journalism, teaching, or carpentry. It doesn't have to be a vocational change, and, as in Bryan's case, it may simply demand reentry with a new list of priorities. Our traditional expectations of a pastor must be scrutinized. As the minister, you may be the one to insist on the changes.

When you are able to assess your own gifts and interests, and develop avenues which utilize them, exciting and creative ministries will emerge. Jesus said that his burden is light and his yoke is easy, and those who discover the meaning of call in terms of their own uniqueness affirm that promise. Those who don't, struggle under a wearisome weight and wonder what's wrong.

Whose yoke are you wearing?

2

Called: by Whom?

Not only must we ask the question, "Called to what?" but also, "By whom?" Moses' call came in the isolation of a desert, and in the improbable guise of a burning bush. Isaiah was worshiping alone. Elijah heard the Lord in a low murmuring sound. Job, in a tempest. Andrew, Peter, James, and John, casting nets; Levi, collecting taxes; and Paul, traveling with a squad of soldiers. God did a pretty decent job of recruiting back in those days.

Has God changed or have we just decided to take over the enlistment office? Now we frequently pack a youth camp auditorium with eager adolescents, produce a high level of emotionalism with lights and sounds, expose the raw and bleeding wounds of mankind, and appeal to our audience for a commitment. In this fashion, many are "called." One young minister told me that at that point in his life he would have volunteered for anything. He really had no idea what he was surrendering to. Could it be that we are sometimes overzealous in impressing on our youth the opportunities in a church vocation? I believe this area of our tradition should be thoughtfully and prayerfully reevaluated. Perhaps out of our own lack of faith and patience we too often *seduce* young people into the services of our churches rather than waiting for God to call them into his service. I believe more caution and less pressure should be applied in our enlistment efforts. I am confident that God is still capable of speaking quietly to those who seek his direction.

Other Voices

Other voices also blend with that of the church to exert their influence "for God." I often hear stories like this one about "Miss Nellie." She was a sweet, kind, and well-meaning stalwart of the church in a small midwestern community. Probably she has little recollection of an event that happened fifteen years ago. Jim was twelve then and had the reputation of being a "holy terror." He was constantly seeking attention and approval through his mischief. One fateful day Miss Nellie remarked in exasperation that the Lord must be calling Jim to his service. Why else would Jim be so full of rebellion and meanness? To Jim, God had just spoken. There could be no question about it. If Miss Nellie, the most righteous and spiritual person he knew, said so, it must be true.

Jim is now out of seminary, but still not free from his inner need to gain acceptance and affirmation, even by rebellion. Through his rebellion he is still testing those important to him. Will they still love him if he behaves badly? Or perhaps the question is, will they pay any attention at all if he doesn't misbehave? I have no idea whether or not God called Jim. I only know that Miss Nellie did.

"Miss Nellie" may be mother, father, aunt, grandmother, pastor, teacher, great-uncle Harry, or anyone else who shows enough interest to say, "You ought to be a preacher," to someone he loves.

The voices may come from within the self rather than from important others. Sometimes this is truly the urging of the Holy Spirit, and sometimes it's not. There are other voices from within that call out to us. To distinguish between them, it is imperative to recognize that much of our motivation is based on unconscious feelings, such as fear, guilt, and self-doubt.

The Fear of Dependency

Let's look first at a common fear, the fear of dependency.[1] A component of this discomfort with one's own emotional needs—this compelling need for independence—is an uncertainty about self-worth. The experience at Interpreter's House [2] has emphasized the almost universal lack of self-esteem carried by the clergy. This combination of anxiety

---

[1] See also Part III.

[2] Interpreters' House is an interdenominational center for dialogue between ministers where participants seek a better understanding of themselves and their call. Dr. Carlyle Marney, a theologian, Dr. Mark Rouch, a theological educator, and Dr. Dan Zeluff, a psychologist, staff the Center at Lake Junaluska, North Carolina.

about dependency with poor self-esteem is practically inevitable. When the developing child is told, "Go away and don't bother me," another message is felt: "You are not worth my time. You are not of value." Hence the child not only becomes frustrated by his current needs and learns to avoid them, he also comes to doubt his individual worth.

One common attempt to gain a sense of self-worth is through dedication to an altruistic vocation such as the ministry. An achievement-oriented life style, often accompanied by a high degree of "success," characterizes these individuals. They go through adulthood trying to win the approval they missed as children. Their honors fail to give them the longed-for glow of satisfaction and acceptance. In one group at Marble Retreat [3] there was a prominent young minister still climbing his ladder to success. At one point in therapy he choked back tears as he told us of trying in every way he could to get his father to say, "I'm proud of you, son." It never happened. Regrettably, his self-worth had been waiting hopefully for those magic words of parental approval which never came. His denominational successes were hollow or only temporarily fulfilling. From the crest of each new honor he slipped back into despair as the inner voice returned, "You've got to do more to prove you can do it—by yourself."

The Guilt Complex

Closely akin to the persistent fear of dependency is an underlying sense of guilt. Maybe you've heard a still, small voice saying, "You no-good, lousy sinner, shape up or ship out!" What do you do with that? Do you sink to depths of depression in a whirlpool of guilt? Since none of us achieves perfection or righteousness, we are all vulnerable to guilt. Individuals who experience little forgiveness and mercy in their lives either become embittered and defensive, or they work harder toward becoming "sinless." Such guilt-ridden persons often devote themselves to answering the call of their over-developed conscience (in psychiatric terms, a punitive superego). The voice of this punishing superego may urge atonement for their sins—or those of their fathers. Could

---

[3] Marble Retreat is a psychotherapy center in Carbondale, Colorado, exclusively for ministers and their families.

there be a more appropriate vocation for this task than serving God? This kind of calling combines a legalistic and perfectionistic struggle that offers little chance of self-fulfillment or acceptance of grace. Paul's struggle with the wretched man inside is a picture of this endless turmoil. The answer Paul found in Christ's forgiveness and healing is drowned out by that incessant voice, "Do better."

This voice of conscience may be aroused by a wide range of experiences. Common causes of guilt are: failure to live up to the expectations of others, various sexual activities which have been forbidden, and unacceptable thoughts and impulses (even though not acted upon).

Ministers sometimes accept the impossible assignment of being omnipotent. Thus they are often prime targets for the guilt derived from letting someone down, of failing. There are many people quite willing to add to the pain as they vent their bitterness or try to control it by provoking guilt. Such reactions as "Where were you when we needed you?" are not unusual. This same technique is used by some parents and can burden the child with a lifelong load of guilt, and even contribute to his vocational choice.

About a year ago I received a call from a minister in the southwest who had suffered from recurrent depression. He inquired about coming for therapy, but twice cancelled appointments. Each time some emergency in his pastorate forced him to stay at home. When he finally made it, I met a sad and angry man overwhelmed by guilt. The pattern had started with his domineering mother who had controlled him by her standard guilt-provoking remark, "How can you do that and hurt your dear mother so?" She had him so well conditioned, he hardly dared go to the bathroom without her approval! She chose his vocation by creating a load of guilt that only complete self-sacrifice could absolve. Unfortunately, even his most dedicated efforts weren't enough—he could never be good enough.

Sexual Problems

Guilt may also be generated by perfectly normal sexual behavior which has been decried as terrible sin within the individual's culture. Masturbation, which is a normal occurrence in the maturation process, particularly in boys, is one example. As the adolescent male begins to experience erections it is difficult to imagine that he would never discover the pleasurable experience of achieving climax. Nowhere does the Bible teach that masturbation is wrong. The story in Genesis of Onan "spilling his seed on the ground" refers to coitus interruptus, not masturbation. Onan disobeyed the clear command of God that he take his brother's widow to wife to raise up a family for his brother.

Another example of supposed sexual sin is that of lustfulness. Looking at an attractive woman lustfully implies more than an appreciation of her beauty, or even a fantasized sexual encounter. To lust after her also entails being consumed by this passion to the point of plotting out or working toward seduction. This distinction is important. To label sexual attraction as adulterous in terms of the Sermon on the Mount is to invite frequent guilt trips for most men. On the other hand, to nurture a passion for girl-watching may move one closer to lustfulness, just as unchecked greed may lead to stealing through dishonest business dealings.

There are some religious groups who extend this disapproval of sexuality to the extreme. Their rigid moralism has fostered in their youth the impression that the sexual drives of the "natural" man are unholy or demonic. They miss the message of creation, denying the marvelous beauty of these God-given desires. Rather than teach the appropriate use of sex in a mature marriage commitment, they admonish against any sacred view of physical relationships. All the time the church is saying, "No," the biological forces of adolescence are saying, "Let's go!" At age twelve or fourteen those charged-up hormones beginning to make the scene haven't the foggiest notion that they are evil. They just keep coming. The resolution of the guilt may be through denial and reaction formation, i.e., the ego says in effect, "I don't have those dirty thoughts, and to prove it I will demonstrate my holiness by becoming a clergyman." That defense, even wrapped up in the trappings of the church, cannot contain normal sexual drive, which will continue to reassert itself. Yet that unconscious psychological maneuver is often an important element in the "call" to the ministry.

Father John is a priest who was raised in just such a right-eous environment. He became a rigidly-controlled boy, hor-rified at the angry feelings he sometimes felt toward his parents. After months of agony and guilt, he began to confess these sins. The temporary relief he felt through confession and penance became a frequent necessity for his peace of mind. So protective was the church that he finally sought permanent escape from his inordinate guilt by entering the priesthood.

Self-doubt

Besides experiencing fear and guilt, a person may be moti-vated by self-doubt. Doubt of one's masculinity is not an un-common aspect of this problem. A sexual identity crisis usually manifests itself most threateningly during adolescence, when vocational choice is being worked out. In the face of such doubt, withdrawal into the feminine subculture of mother church may seem to be a solution. This safer environment may only postpone the confrontation with the doubt. The underlying question as to one's maleness may be deep-seated and hard to relieve. Any situation that threatens one's potency may reawaken the anxiety. For instance, trouble in marital or family relationships, or in the administrative stresses of the pastorate, can nurture the doubt. Not only does this create anxiety, but it may also lead to sexual activity. It is always embarrassing to the Christian community when a pastor is arrested for indecent exposure, or voyeurism, or molesting a child. All of these may reflect a basic doubt as to the of-fender's maleness and his need to prove that he is potent.

So you see, there are many voices crying out to us, both from the community and from within. They must be identi-fied so that their unconscious dominance may be overcome. Only then may God's voice be heard. He does still speak. He calls us to healthy commitment of self, a *self* worth giving back to him. I know of no other way to follow Christ but by total surrender in an hour-by-hour commitment of will. De-ciding the personal "pulpit" we must fill is another task. That decision needs to be made under conditions as free as possible from neurotic pressures or institutional recruitment.

3

Called: to Freedom and Fulfilment

Twenty-four years ago, as an awkward, unsettled adolescent, I responded to "God's call." Many others, before and since, have done the same. How was that "call" validated? How can one determine, even for himself, much less for another, what differentiates God's call from all the other voices? What does a man do when he begins to realize he is not in the place God has for him? How can we lead the community of believers into a growing sensitivity to God's calling out of each person?

I can speak most authoritatively about God's call to *me* and the pilgrimage that has resulted. A degree of objectivity will be sacrificed as I use my own experience to show how one hears the call, but I think it can still help us discover some guidelines.

My Experience

For several years I assumed that my calling was to the pastorate, and I rejected any other idea. As I progressed through high school my interest and abilities in drama brought me the first serious doubts about preaching as a vocation. Fortunately I had open-minded Christian teachers who showed me the potential for Christian witness through theater and the dramatic arts. I was soon convinced that my service was to be as a Christian actor and playwright. A whole new world of ministry opened before my eyes. Excited and delighted that God was going to use a skill He had given me, I applied for a scholarship and enrolled in college.

Then came the first closed door—I received no response to my scholarship application. I had been rejected by those I thought should recognize my dramatic ability. At that point I assumed that I had misinterpreted God's call. I continued taking general required courses, avoiding the drama department which had ignored me (I'd show them), and praying for God's will to be revealed. At this point, surprisingly, I discovered an interest in the premedical curriculum and began to earnestly seek his leading regarding medicine and possibly medical missions. Just as abruptly as the theater door seemed to close, the medical door opened, and I entered with growing enthusiasm. It was only after I had firmly committed myself to this new direction that I was informed by the drama department of the secretarial error which was responsible for my not being notified of my full scholarship in drama. I wish I knew that secretary. I'd give her a big hug!

Medical school went smoothly, and now that I was married, there were two of us who sought God's ultimate direction— apparently medical missions. Then Dr. Shervert Frazier came to Baylor Medical College as the new chairman of psychiatry. A dynamic Christian psychiatrist, he awakened in me an interest in that medical subspecialty. After an internship in internal medicine and experience in general practice in the Navy, I was convinced that psychiatry was where God wanted me, but as a medical missionary? Impossible!

It was not until I was half-way through my specialty training that God began to reveal the next step in the pilgrimage. As God had always done before, he awakened me to a need, the problems of ministers. He gradually affirmed me in my ability to serve in this area, and provided the way for me to walk in this new light. I am a long way from a pastorate, the theater, or medical missions, and yet in this ministry I have the opportunity to use all the gifts and training God has provided. This, I'm convinced, is the peculiar spot and work for which I was prepared. I need no further validation than the walk I have made thus far, and the light he has given.

The Call

In a more objective way, what can be said about "call"? The first principle is that God has called each of us to a unique and special task. He has also called us to common tasks and equipped us by interest and ability to seize the opportunities that open to us. The Bible clearly teaches that each of us has spiritual gifts, and experience confirms this. Not only are there many parts of Christ's body, the church, but within the ordained ministry is a vast range of possibilities for the individual to express his uniqueness. One minister may excel as a teacher, but dislike the burden of his pastoral duties. A second may fail miserably as an expository preacher, but be sensitive and effective as a counselor. I don't think God intends each of us to do all things well, but rather he desires that we serve him with the gifts he has given.

Mark's Experience

Several years ago I knew a minister who lived through a serious crisis related to his own uniqueness. A dedicated, concerned, and sympathetic man, Mark has been a pastor for many years. He is an excellent counselor and pastor to his people. In the context of a close relationship or teaching one or two people, he speaks with wisdom and authority. The sermons he writes are well thought out, and his theses persuasively supported. His depth and breadth of knowledge are impressive. But Mark is embarrassingly uncomfortable and inept as a public speaker. He completely lacks any ability to motivate a congregation and induce enthusiasm. He had seriously questioned his calling and was ready to resign when he was called to a pastorate where his natural abilities could be used maximally. In his new situation his weakness was minimized by using other church leaders for public speaking and organizational expertise. He is now happily convinced of God's "call."

One conclusion I have reached from Mark's experience, as well as Paul's teaching, is that we must utilize many "ministers" in the body. All too often we relegate all the tasks to the pastor who then tries to "do it all," often failing bitterly.

In *Eighth Day of Creation* Elizabeth O'Connor speaks convincingly about our individual giftedness and the satisfaction that comes from discovering our uniqueness. At Redstone, Colorado, a neighbor of mine, Jim Denton, is answering

God's call to him by helping others in retreat to discover their gifts. It is an exciting ministry of liberation.

A second guideline for finding God's call is the meshing of ability, training, and opportunity. When a committed Christian places his life in God's hands he will find doors of service opening, in which he can utilize his talents and education. It is not coincidental that some golden opportunities are suddenly withdrawn while other completely unexpected ones appear. In her book, *L'Abri*, Edith Schaeffer tells of remarkable experiences in Switzerland which demonstrate God's working and his call in this way.

Charlie's Experience

An important point to remember is to follow God's leadership and not run ahead as Charlie did. He was a seminary student who decided he was tired of academics and was ready to serve on the front lines.

Although only a year before he had felt convinced the Lord had placed him in seminary and given him that opportunity for training, he dropped out of school and entered his first pastorate. It soon proved to be a nightmare. He found himself ill-prepared to deal with the interpersonal problems within the congregation, and unable to lead toward unity and cooperation. I don't know if completing his degree program would have assured Charlie's handling the problems he faced, but I do believe he had begun to run ahead of the Lord's leading. After his baptism of fire, he may have learned a lesson. I hope so.

Those traumatic pastorates are far too common, but I don't believe God leads us into situations destructive to his body. Frequently it is the impatience of a pulpit committee that brings about the mismatch of minister and people, but not always. The impatience of an individual may push him into a job situation that he knows full well he is not equipped to fill, either by training or ability.

An Awareness of Need

Finally, a further indication of "call" is the keen awareness of a need that God impresses upon a person, sometimes in an incredible way. The world has more needs (physical, spiritual, and emotional) than any of us can begin to fathom, much less effectively meet. Yet somehow my pastor, Randy Foster, has been shown the spiritual hunger of the Roaring Fork Valley of Colorado, while Dr. Martha Gilliland, a missionary surgeon, cannot evade the human suffering of Nigeria. Ron Willis dedicates his life and ministry to the street people of San Antonio, whereas Keith Miller has found a spiritual vacuum in the lives of America's executives and professionals. I could go on and on.

Try to interest any of these individuals in the ministry of the others, and only a general acknowledgment of the need is made. In fact, there may be a discouraging and even maddening coolness as each of us tries to share his own burden with the world. A wonderful friend of mine, Doug Dillard, shared an invaluable insight with me when I enthusiastically told him of my "call" to Marble Retreat. He said simply, "Don't be surprised if everyone doesn't share your exuberance—it's your private hurt."

What does one do when "his private hurt" becomes an unbearable burden, when the yoke is uneasy and fulfilment denied? I think the first step is to admit the pain and doubt to self. We may have to say, "Maybe this isn't where God wants me after all." This is the hardest step, for it seems to threaten a deep and significant aspect of "selfhood." There are the prospects of rejection by others who have encouraged us, and a sense of failure as we admit we aren't happy. There looms the threat to our faith, since we believed firmly that God was leading and in control. We must also face the uncertainty that change of direction might entail. However, once this confession is made to self, it becomes less threatening to share it with someone else.

At this point it is imperative to reevaluate the original "call" in terms of the voices we have just discussed. Did I enter the ministry simply to gain the approval of my parents or pastor? Was my call based on unconscious guilt or fears? Was I recruited by a smooth-talking salesman, or did I respond to God's claim on my life? These issues must be settled.

If God really called and not "Miss Nellie," * then to what was he calling? Here is where an understanding of one's own uniqueness is critical. Was I pushed into a traditional mold as I responded to his call? Are there areas of service for which I am better equipped by ability or interest? Are there ways I can reorganize my ministry in my present position to better utilize my potential?

Listening to God

These questions may need to be asked during a period of withdrawal from the pressure of daily life. The help and counsel of a colleague, or a professional placement center, may be useful. It is certainly necessary to spend time listening in silence to God. We have become so embroiled in the chaotic noise of living that we seldom *listen* to God. Even in prayer, most of us do all the talking. I was telling a friend about my "call" and how God had answered prayers in searching out his will. He responded with surprise and near disbelief, "It's been a long time since I made any decision in the context of prayer."

This decision-making and reevaluation process is not painless! On the contrary, it may be the most difficult course of action one ever takes. The rewards are significant as one finds himself settling into the freedom of the promise of the easy yoke. God may be leading right back into the place you just left, but under different expectations and with rearranged priorities. It may be he wants to change *you*, not your place of service.

On the other hand, the change may need to be made in the community you serve. The traditions we honor are often slow to change. Frequently they have outlasted their usefulness long before we discard them. The subject of "call" is one such tradition. We must reeducate the Christian community to the concept of call to each individual. This process will accomplish two important goals. First, it will emphasize and demand

---

* See Chapter 2.

individual commitment by every Christian, removing the option of spectator Christianity. Second, as each member of the body of Christ finds his gifts and develops them, it will free all other members to function in the specific area of their calling. No longer will the hand have to try to do the work of the tongue, ear, and left big toe—no longer will the pastor have to be teacher, evangelist, business manager, and janitor. Furthermore, every calling will come to be respected, honored, and appreciated.

I am encouraged as I read, travel, and observe the church in the United States today. I find a reawakening of commitment, an increased sensitivity to the call to involvement. The Christian call is an exciting, challenging demand on our life —every aspect of it. It is a call not only to service, but to freedom and fulfilment. Take this message to your heart and to your people.

Part II

The Encumbered

And what of ourselves? With all these witnesses to faith around us like a cloud, we must throw off every encumbrance, every sin to which we cling, and run with resolution the race for which we are entered . . . (Heb. 12:1 NEB).

My children have been organizing a spook house this afternoon. Melissa, my wife, cut eye-holes in an old sheet—instant ghost. Our youngest son, Brent, was terrifying (and terrified). An old black raincoat transformed our daughter, Andrea, into a horrible old witch. Bruce, our oldest son, has the entire neighborhood organized and mobilized in the neighbor's garage. I paid my nickel and got the treatment. One bedsheet ghost leaped and shrieked from behind a blanket, a reluctant Martian peeked from the attic, and then remembered his mask, hastily retreating to reemerge with a growl. A couple of boxes bounced around as if alive. One rather cute witch cackled threateningly, and the lifeless form of a small boy lay fallen from his bicycle with his chest (or armpit) pierced by an arrow, which only moved slightly with each excited breath.

All in all, it was the best deal I've made for a nickel in a long time. When I went business was slow, but it has since picked up considerably. Every half hour or so I hear a great scurry of feet and Bruce shouts, "Everybody get ready. We've got some customers coming." Then I can imagine the action in the garage while everyone suits up and gets into position for the gathering crowd. Reminds me of a bunch of physicians leaving the doctors' lounge to present themselves to waiting patients. White coats go on, stethoscopes are readied, dignity and professionalism are donned like so many masks. Even the sounds we utter carry the appropriate muffled solemnity and knowing sighs. We all play our roles so well! It is interesting to watch the children practice for adulthood.

Of all the professional people I know, none is more sensitive to the expectations of the crowd than the minister. Many in religious vocations wear outward symbols to identify themselves, but even those who don't can frequently be recognized as men of the cloth. I once suspected that seminaries had classes in fitting the ministerial image, but have since discovered that they don't. The minister learns his part by watching his peers, identifying with his teachers, and most critically, responding to the expectations of the "witnesses."

Let's examine the expectations most ministers feel and how they are communicated.

At the outset I want to make one point clear. It is not all bad to be attuned to the expectations of our environment and to try to meet them. In fact, much of our personality formation and identity depends on incorporation of cultural demands. It is only when the values included in our conscience (superego) and the goals we have adopted as part of our idealized self-image (ego ideal) are unrealistic that being sensitive to the requirements becomes detrimental.

Many Christians who require psychiatric treatment have developed conflicts in one of these two areas of personality and identity. They are overwhelmed by guilt and feelings of unworthiness. Their conscience has been overdeveloped to the point of constantly reminding them of their sinfulness. Their ego ideal insists on perfection. No room is left for failure and God's grace. Atonement is still being worked out rather than being accepted as a gift from the Father. They labor under a heavy burden of never being able to live up to the severe standards they have embraced out of early needs for acceptance. An exasperating cycle is set up: attempt perfection to gain acceptance, fail, then struggle with a painful sense of rejection. That treadmill isn't much fun. What are the expectations you've accepted that keep you trudging along getting nowhere? Let's look at some of the usual ones.

You may spot yourself stumbling under the weight of some of these burdens. For a few minutes, at least, put the bundles down, get off the merry-go-round, and relax.

4

Availability

A close friend of mine pastors a church of several thousand members. Not long ago we were discussing the problems he faces. He headed his list with the demands on his time and the ruthless invasion of his privacy. "Louis," he confided almost apologetically, "I have to disappear one day a week and not let anyone know where I'm going to be. If I didn't, I'd have no time to myself, and I really need it for my own sanity." There are times, of course, when members of his church become irritated with him because he is unavailable, even though they understand his need for privacy. Consequently, he has had to be highly resolved to continue the practice and not always try to meet the expectations of being available all day, every day.

You are probably well aware that the "urgent" needs of those who depend on you are often trivial. For example, my children often demonstrate the basic pattern of "checking in," which is what many "emergencies" represent. They burst into the house, slamming doors, and yelling for mother with all the urgency of a major disaster. Melissa responds only to find they have forgotten why they even came in. This is a universal behavior of dependency which satisfies the need for security. "Am I going to be cared for?" "Is mother still around?"

When I was the general medical officer for a Naval Communication Station, I frequently answered "emergency" calls which were about as critical as our children's requests for a drink of water. Similarly, you pastors spend much of your time reassuring your people that "daddy really cares." I believe this demand that the minister be available at all times is unrealistic.

The primary problem in this area is that of the dependency needs of the people. You must gently educate them to accept you as a human being and to realize your needs. They may want to cling to the comfortable fantasy of having a symbolic father who is always there to calm their fears and soothe their hurts. It is at the times of fears and hurts that the little child within all of us is most likely to take control and demand a parent. That child can learn to yield to the reason and maturity of adulthood. He must either face the discomfort alone or consider your needs as pastor before intruding on your privacy. Most demands of this kind may safely be delayed.

Another obstacle to freeing yourself from this unreasonable demand lies inside yourself. The problem is this: the fear of rejection if it is ever discovered you can't be there all the time. It is important to realize the absolutely impossible task you have accepted—whether you are shepherding a flock of fifty or five thousand! Impossible. Jesus chose twelve to disciple, and he wasn't always available even to them. You will discover that your flock will understand, will grant you some space for yourself and your family, and will learn to depend on undershepherds in the body, mature Christians who are chosen for this pastoral ministry. They may be able to do the job better than you could anyway. Does that threaten you? It does most of us. We feel we must be in control to be considered indispensable. That introduces the second burden most ministers carry—the need to be "able."

5

Ability

At times it is difficult to decide whether the expectations you respond to are primarily from others or from within yourself. Whereas the notion that the pastor must always be on call can be attributed mainly to the people, the equally demanding requirement of being "able" to do all things arises from within. As with all emotion, there is a broad spectrum of intensity involved in this inner striving for competence. It is quite normal and even admirable to attain a level of excellence in what you do. Not uncommonly, though, I see individuals who have adopted such lofty standards it is quite impossible to reach them.

Ministers frequently fall into this category. Your ego ideal allows no margin for error or inability. Although most of us realize there are things we can't do and things we don't know, ministers don't generally let this mark of humanity show. It would appear that they fear complete rejection should one area of weakness be discovered. Instead, they try to be all things: teacher, speaker, counselor, administrator, evangelist, etc. Paul assured us that we all have certain spiritual gifts, but he emphasized equally that no person would be blessed with all gifts.

Last year a pastor attending a seminar confessed he had never been able to say, "I don't know," or "I can't." He found it easier to fake it, at times making up an answer rather than telling the truth. Needless to say, this practice frequently backfired, and his personal credibility gap was a growing problem. He was relieved to discover that he could finally shed the burden of such unrealistic expectations, and he has since become much more open, friendly, and at peace with himself.

His most pleasant surprise has been the acceptance he feels from his parishioners even when he doesn't have all the answers.

This inner need to be able to do all things and know all things is directly related to one's insecurity. When an individual is uncertain about his capability, he must be extremely careful not to reveal his deficiency. This is clearly demonstrated in the medical profession. The medical student who is serving in his first hospital is scared to death and knows practically nothing about caring for a sick human being. He is so insecure he is uncomfortable asking anyone anything. He won't even ask the nurse what time it is.

The intern, who has his medical degree and two more years of experience in patient care, is slightly less fearful, but he still retains a reasonable discomfort about being "Doctor Smith." At least, he may be able to ask another intern the dose of some medicine, if he doesn't remember for sure.

The resident, now settled into his special field of interest, older and more confident, is free to expose his lack of knowledge much more freely. He can even ask the nurse, "What's a good laxative for Mr. Jones?"

The consultant physician with twenty years of practice, who has long since learned he is competent but doesn't know everything, strides up to the nurses' station and asks, "Mary, what's wrong with Mrs. Wagner in 421?"

So it is in the ministry. When you are a young pastor fresh out of seminary, you must maintain tight control and have a hard time admitting you don't know everything and can't do it all. As you grow more comfortable and secure within yourself, this need to be omnipotent fades out. The remarkable thing is that you become much more believable as a human being and more approachable by your congregation.

6

Sinlessness

A few months ago I was talking on the phone to a minister with whom I have had a very short acquaintance. When we first met, we both felt that instant attraction and warmth toward each other that sometimes happens. Recognizing it, as I had, he suggested, "We've got to get together sometime. I bet we could have a great time—might even air our dirty linen." For an ordained minister there could be no deeper indication of trust. In effect he was saying, "I think you will accept me even if I am not morally perfect." I considered that a great compliment, for ministers usually keep up their masks of righteousness and piety at all costs. It is expected.

You can locate the source of this expectation both in the congregation and in the clergy. The flock holds out for perfection in part because the church, and you as her spokesman, have assumed the role of moral watchdog. There is often a much greater emphasis on law and judgment than on grace and forgiveness. The people then expect you, their community conscience, to practice what you preach. Thus it is that the flock can be comfortable with a sort of ecclesiastical double standard which finds forgiveness for an errant brother, but swift and certain judgment for the sinners who happen to be ordained.

Of course there is some justification for us to expect our ministers to commit themselves daily to putting God's kingdom first. Although Jesus said, "Neither do I condemn thee," he also said, "Go and sin no more." As a pastor, you are not and should not be exempt from that command. But when you as a minister fail to live up to that commandment, you should find forgiveness from God and the *other* sinners who comprise

the church—as well as from yourself. The first source of forgiveness, the Father, is assured; the second, the people, is not
so certain; and the third, yourself, may be the most difficult
of all.

As with the expectations of availability and ability, an understanding attitude by the congregation must be a matter of
education, and that is a long process. How do you ever learn
to forgive yourself?

The freedom from continuous self-condemnation will depend essentially on what expectations you carry. You may
share the ideal of sinless perfection. The danger in subscrib-
ing to this standard is that it is often seen as a description of
the Christian rather than a goal toward which he strives. In
Search for Silence Elizabeth O'Connor points out that as believers we have not achieved perfection, but are striving for it.
The church, she says, is a group in the process of "getting
houses off sand and onto the rock." Without that viewpoint
it may be impossible to deal effectively with the failure to attain the ideal, and you may be caught up in the "wretched
man that I am" syndrome, never accepting forgiveness from
any source.

A particularly sad situation is that of those of you who enter
the ministry to remove yourself from the temptations of "the
world." To seek protection from temptation behind a pulpit
is inviting disaster, for only the anticipation of a sinless life
awaits the seminarian—not its realization. The most restric-
tive, secluded monastery cannot remove sin, for self is always
with us and self is the root of sin.

7

Emotional Self-Sufficiency and Invulnerability

Perhaps the most destructive and dehumanizing of all ridiculous notions about pastors is that you have no emotional needs. People expect you to be a thickskinned automaton as they criticize and abuse, but if they are hurting, you are to be warm and comforting. This expectation probably survives because most clergymen are afraid to admit their own vulnerability. You accept the challenge to be supermen, and in pursuit of that goal you rigidly conceal your feelings.

I see evidence of this regularly on three different levels. As I visit congregations, I am often aware of turmoil in the life of the minister, or internal strife between the staff and the congregation, yet smiles and back-slapping prevail. I suppose I can understand the desire to keep up appearances if for no other reason than simply not to air dirty linen in front of visitors. One can't have prospective members aware of conflict.

The second level I see is less understandable. I have frequent occasion to speak to groups of ministers, both interdenominational groups and those of the same doctrinal persuasion. One would expect that here a clergyman in pain could surely unburden and feel the support and acceptance of his peers, men who have experienced many of his hurts. Not so! The masks stay on.

Finally, I counsel ministers who have come to Marble Retreat because of emotional problems. Even in this retreat setting with the avowed purpose of getting help, they take several hours before they begin to share their feelings. The expectation has been solidly established—clergymen have no hurts; they do not cry or become angry; and for many of them even to show love is difficult.

In a recent conference, one minister elatedly reported that he had just discovered he could share his true feelings with his people without rejection. He realized he had been expressing his resentment, fears, and frustration only through his sermons. You should have seen the smile on his face. What joy he had found in his new relationship with the congregation!

Another pastor I know was telling me about his struggle with depression. He reached the point of desperation where he simply couldn't keep up the front. When that finally happened, and his people sensed his despair, they rallied to his support. He had tears in his eyes as he told me of their love.

8

Renunciation of Material Needs

During a year of study in London I met with groups of British ministers on several occasions. One brisk autumn day I joined about seventeen clergymen in a delightful fifteenth century abbey. It was exquisite. White clerical collars all about, heavy English accents, a glowing fire, and a richly-paneled room. *What an utterly delightful existence these fellows enjoy,* I was thinking. Then we began to share along the lines of my interest in problems of the ministry. To a man, these Anglican priests and Methodist ministers listed as one of their major problems that of poverty. (Not all men of the cloth take vows of poverty, but frequently this doesn't make any difference. Ministers are the lowest paid professional group in England, as well as in the United States.)

Those British brothers seemed grateful for the opportunity to open up. They felt a twinge of resentment toward their parishioners, who shop at Harrods and vacation in the Alps, while they scrimp and save to afford a week in Devon or Cornwall. Their schoolmates move into comfortable houses, an investment for retirement, while they shuttle about from manse to manse. At the age of 65, they will receive the sincere, heartfelt thanks of their parishioners, a pat on the back, and an eviction notice. If they have been exceptionally frugal they may have accumulated enough savings to take a small retirement apartment and continue the struggle. The situation is not much different in the United States.

Ministers and Materialism

The Lord said, "Lay not up for yourselves treasures on earth," and the church has rallied to the command in behalf of their minister! It is a good thing Paul said "a workman is worthy of his hire," or we'd probably pay nothing at all. Some congregations seem to deeply resent their pastor's having any material needs. It may be that they don't think he really does much work in the first place.

A fascinating corollary to this expectation that the minister get by on next to nothing, is that you must do it in grand style. You must entertain with flair, dress in fashion, and give generously to the United Fund, the Boy Scouts, the Ladies Aid, and the building fund. There's really not much danger that you are going to become overpaid and sin by laying up treasures on earth. There may not even be a serious threat of your receiving a decent wage.

This expectation seems to be shared by pastor and people alike. I've known many ministers who feel guilty about asking for help. From the standpoint of the congregation, it is mostly a matter of ignorance, lack of concern, or shallowness of commitment. You must resolve the internal conflict as you realize your value and become satisfied that the Lord does not intend for you to suffer needlessly. You must then be willing to share with your congregation your physical needs in an orderly, documented way.

Money Management

The problem is compounded if you are a poor money manager and the community is drawn into the picture in some creditor's attempt to collect a bad debt from you. You may begin to feel that because you are so poorly paid the world owes you a living—that you can become financially irresponsible and expect the church to bail you out. One minister who came to me for therapy had been in bankruptcy twice, and he complained bitterly of his low salary. His wife worked to help make ends meet and managed the money, or at least tried her best. She was filled with bitterness, too—some of it toward the church, but most of it toward her husband. She would just about get them out of debt, and he would impulsively buy some expensive new toy.

Impulsive buying may reflect various psychological forces.

It may express anger toward one's spouse, church, or the world at large. Many individuals regularly seek relief from depression by buying something new. However, unwise spending may simply be one aspect of total immaturity and inability to delay gratification.

As if all these internal pressures weren't enough, pastors are constantly being attacked by the advertising media. You're constantly bombarded with the *need* to purchase. Credit buying removes the practical barrier of an empty pocketbook and we respond eagerly. The acquisition of "things" has become "the good life" in free America. As a Christian, you have the task of being a wise money manager and committing your financial resources to God. Such a commitment may reduce your wardrobe, or call for denial of some "urgent" desire. The new car, stereo, color TV, camper, boat and motor, power tool, or new suit that you really *need* may have to wait.

There is a middle ground of responsible money management. You don't have to live in poverty, but you must set the example for your people of wise stewardship of material possessions. A money-management conference for your church may open the way for better use of these resources for all your people, and it may open up an opportunity for you to discuss your personal financial requirements with your people.

9

Communicating the Standards

We've looked at several common expectations and demands placed upon the man of God. How are they communicated? Were you to ask your local churches if they require such characteristics, you'd meet adamant denial. If you inspected the job description or contracts of your friends in the ministry, no such "expectation" clauses would appear. Nonetheless we have seen that both sides of the pulpit seem to make these demands, and even accept them as valid. Somehow the message is getting through.

By Tradition

The first mode of transmission is through tradition. The common image of preacher or priest is passed along through literature, drama, and the day-to-day display in community life. The image is enforced within our seminaries and institutional structures. Though each age may leave the stamp of its personality, generation after generation falls in line, eager to be accepted within the peer group. No element of society is free from this pressure.

The most striking example I know is the current flock of nonconformists. These ragged individualists denounce the "establishment" and supposedly resist being shoved into some mold. Carefully uniformed in denim and hair, they rigorously defend their individualism. We are all in the same boat—supremely sensitive to the demands of our culture. The ecclesiastical subculture is no exception.

These demands are communicated by the examples of tradition. My son Bruce learned how to act the sandlot baseball player by watching a few games. Then the cap becomes tilted casually and "attababy" chatters out just right. So it is with standing in the "dugout" at the church—we learn the appropriate uniform and jargon.

It began when you were children and heard your parents and their friends discuss the preacher. The conversations you heard must have caused some initial confusion. You saw the smiles and handshakes in the foyer and heard the sincere compliments on the sermon. Then in the car on the way home from church the criticism began. It may well have lasted until next Sunday morning.

You saw the minister set apart, treated differently, and often in a phony sort of way. When the pastor came for a visit, the house took on a sudden sanctified air. The Bible came out of hiding, the usual magazines may have disappeared along with the alcoholic beverages (in some circles), and the language—especially the language—changed. The topics of conversation, the word choices, and even the tone and inflections became "religious." The image was set. Ministers are holy, special, not-quite-human beings. There is little wonder that expectations become so warped.

Then as you grew up you became gradually more aware of how the minister spoke and acted. He fit into those early impressions, and most of your exposures confirmed the image. He was treated with polite respect but seemed to lack close friends. In most of his relationships he was the "pray-er." I've heard many ministers bemoan the fact that all they are asked to do is pronounce benedictions at the Rotary Club. They feel unheard in the give-and-take of real life. However, they do receive a certain respect for position as a compensation.

The young man who has committed himself to study theology will find a pattern for his behavior among ministers he knows and through seminary training. In homiletics he learns the forms his communications must take; the language and inflection he picks up by imitation. This communication style is extremely important.

A few years ago I became acquainted with a young pastor who was having some growing pains in a very nontraditional —in fact almost antitraditional—church. He was a warm, personable, concerned person. Then I visited his church and saw a subtle transformation. His speech became polished, professional, and "ministerial." Although that style may have been valued elsewhere, we were able to identify it as the "phoniness" many of his church members found offensive. *He* wasn't phony, but his sermon delivery *was*.

Let me put it another way. I have a friend who is a new Christian. He recently made us all aware of the change in our verbal communication when we were being "religious." At church one day he said, "I'm not comfortable praying in public because I don't know all the 'heavenly sunshine' words." Sometimes it is the "heavenly sunshine" vocabulary that dehumanizes the preacher. (However, I don't think you must adopt gutter-language to prove your manliness and humanity. I think that current movement is a little extreme and adolescent.)

So you see there are many ways the preacher-image is passed on, first through the family, then through the pulpit, and finally through the religious community. Furthermore, the fellowship of believers devises many special techniques for transmitting its influence.

By 'the Oblique Thrust'

One of the interesting communication techniques of the religious community is what I call "the oblique thrust." It's the curious way we have devised to avoid direct confrontation. We're so afraid of anger and conflict that we go to ridiculous extremes to disguise our dissatisfaction or opinions. Thus, instead of Elder Smith approaching you and discussing a disagreement directly with you, his message is delivered obliquely or behind your back. Some of the most destructive hostility to be found anywhere oozes its way through the aisles and into both pulpit and pews of our sanctuaries. We smile and greet each other with holy kisses until backs are turned—then look out! If any attempt at all is made toward confrontation, it is a weakly veiled suggestion, laden with double meaning.

I was recently discussing this problem with a minister who readily recognized the pattern but said he chooses to ignore such criticism. I'm afraid, though, that the communique can't be completely ignored. The oblique thrust has been delivered and the wound felt, smiles notwithstanding. What's more, the expectation has been levied. "I'd like for you . . ."; "I'm disappointed that you didn't . . ." etc. The minister usually plays the game and responds with the same sort of statement. Confrontation is avoided, but conflict and destructive anger are perpetuated. With all the cloudiness of this form of communication, it becomes apparent why frequent misunderstandings occur.

By Direct Verbalization

Fortunately, there is another way of communicating your thoughts. They may be directly verbalized. It is cleaner and less complicated to respond to an open, honest message. If I come to you and say, "I disagreed with your interpretation of the scripture this morning. Can we discuss it?" there is an invitation to dialogue. The opportunity is opened for us to share opposing views and for each of us to learn. You will frequently help me to a new understanding of some theological point, and I think at times it may work the other way around. I may say, "I'd like for you to do such and such," and you can say, "I don't want to. Why don't you?" To me that is more honest than for me to coerce you with "The Lord has told me we need to be more active in thus and so," and for you to respond, "I'll just wait for his leading. Let's pray about it, brother."

I think you must make every effort to understand how the expectations are placed upon you, and what they are. Then perhaps you can begin to lay aside the weights that have become so cumbersome, and start to run.

Part III

Common Problems and a

Common Psychological

Base

He called a child, set him in front of them and said, "I tell you this, unless you turn around and become like children you will never enter the kingdom of Heaven" (Matt. 18:3 NEB).

Not many men turn around and become as little children. To do so brings them face to face with pain and doubt, for in childhood we experience the discomfort that comes with being dependent on others to meet our needs, and with surrendering our own authority. In fact, at the core of many problems faced by clergymen are unresolved conflicts over authority and dependency.

The "ideal" childhood allows a comfortable dependency on a secure and reliable authority figure. Independence is encouraged and new freedom granted in the gradual process of maturation. Adulthood is reached with an inner sense of acceptance, and dependency can be admitted without feeling inadequate. Since we all need other people physically and emotionally, it's an advantage to be able to live comfortably with our dependency. Unfortunately, the ideal childhood is often compromised.

I suspect those of you who are parents have wished sometimes that you could become invisible to escape the demands of your children. There have certainly been times when I've wanted to vanish, but I never have discovered the secret of disappearing—physically. Instead, I just withdraw mentally and emotionally, or tell my children not to bother me. I'm particularly prone to do this when I first come in after a busy day or a tiring trip—the very time they most need my attention. This is such a common problem for us parents. More often than not, we disappear or tell our child to wait.

The youngster exposed to repeated refusals and rebuffs must either try harder to be heard or simply shut up. In either instance, his needs remain unmet and become the source of unpleasant feelings. These feelings may be pushed out of his consciousness, but they remain in the unconscious to impinge on *all future relationships*. The defenses employed to avoid the discomfort vary. Grown men "rationalize" that it is a sign of weakness to admit needs, or fears, or hurts (i.e., big boys don't cry). The feeling of being unworthy and a bother to others creates a deep-seated rage which may be directed toward self, "introjected," with resultant guilt and depression (i.e., what a terrible person I am to demand love and attention), or toward others in "projection and paranoia" (i.e., everyone is against me and trying to hurt me). "Reaction formation" is the psychological means of not only denying one's own feelings, but adopting the exact opposite stance (i.e., I have no needs and in fact will be a great helper to others). Whatever the mode of defense, the basic discomfort remains. The rejected child still cries out within for love and approval, and may never achieve comfortable adult relationships.

The Authority—Dependency Relationship

Another distinctive pattern of authority and dependency in child development is that of the overly protective, controlling parent who fosters dependency and will not let go. Such a stranglehold ultimately begins to suffocate the child. Not a few ministers play out their role in life as miserable misfits having responded to the demands of a domineering parent rather than the call of God. If selfhood is to be achieved in any meaningful sense, freedom from such a dominating parent must be attained even if it means war. It is a costly war at best. One price is lifelong anxiety whenever dependency or closeness threatens. The self-protective alarm system is tripped and the message sounds out, "Closeness is dangerous. Keep your distance. You may be smothered again."

The authority-dependency relationship may be illustrated with the drawings on the next page which show the three

most common patterns. The first drawing demonstrates the healthy authority dependency relationship which we all crave. As you can see, the authority figure (capital "A") is solid and has a broad base and a long arm, which allows the small dependency figure to slide comfortably away toward independence. Authority figures ideally have the features of strength, consistency, dependability, and an attitude of acceptance and encouragement. Those dependent on such authority feel safe while growing toward autonomy.

The second illustration uses a small "a" to represent the authority figure and to illustrate the insecurity felt by such an individual. This parent has never achieved the comfortable status of adulthood characterized by the capital "A." The dependency figure is shown as almost the same size, illustrating that to the inadequate and insecure parent the dependency needs of the child often seem overwhelming. As may be seen in the drawing, there is not much to lean on in this authority figure. The dependent must cling desperately in order to have his needs met, and he will slide off altogether more quickly and less well prepared than anticipated and desired.

The third illustration represents the overcontrolling, smothering parent shown by an austere Gothic capital "A." Overwhelming the small and insignificant dependency figure carefully contained within, this adult allows no independence or freedom. Thus the child of the controlling and overprotective parent feels imprisoned, a completely dependent part of his parent—and he is insecure about his own ability to function autonomously.

You may be asking what this has to do with the crisis of the clergy. In part, we will see the relationship expressed in the individual personality and childhood experience of the minister, and in part through the relationship between pastor and people. Let's discuss five common problems and relate each to the authority/dependency issue: (1) Chapter 10. Loneliness and Isolation; (2) Chapter 11. Unexpressed Hostility; (3) Chapter 12. A Sense of Failure and Inadequacy; (4) Chapter 13. Job Insecurity; and (5) Chapter 14. Role Confusion.

10

Loneliness and Isolation

Recently I was having lunch with an Episcopalian priest. A warm, outgoing man of middle age, he shared with me an experience of a few years before. He had become disillusioned with his ministry, questioned his calling and commitment, and was at the end of his rope. The most agonizing aspect of his dilemma was having no one with whom he could share his hurt. He felt threatened at the prospect of confiding in a parishioner, he feared that his bishop would blackball him, and he was embarrassed to confess to a colleague. In despair, he simply disappeared to a large city and lost himself for a few days. There, in physical loneliness, he found the peace unavailable in his emotional isolation within the crowd at home. His story was painfully familiar to me.

Ministers are too often lonely men. The prophet has always walked apart from his fellows, but what consuming aloneness he endures. Must it be so? I think not. Even Elijah was reminded by God that he was not alone—that there were seven thousand still faithful. Elijah had isolated himself.

The Pedestal Problem

Why then does this self-induced exile still go on with God's prophets? Part of the isolation can be expressed by the pedestal problem. It is formed both by the people and by the minister's need for distance and isolation. At the psychological root of the pedestal problem is the issue of authority and dependency.

If you are to feel in control (that is to be in authority), you may be convinced you must not be vulnerable. There is some justification for fear on your part that your position of authority may be eroded by closeness to your people, and the resulting exposure of any weakness. In the past fifteen years or so, anyone who presumes to be an authority has been challenged. One way to avoid this erosion of authority is to construct a system of walls around oneself. Unfortunately, those protective barricades also isolate.

The priest I met had begun to question his own authority base, which further threatened his interpersonal relationships and magnified his need for distance. This threat to authority —and hence to authenticity—becomes meaningless when we appropriate Christ's authority. He said, "All authority is given me in heaven and on earth," and "As the heavenly Father sent me even so send I you." We are commissioned not in our own power but in his. And Christ's authority is that perfectly reliable structure that permits comfortable dependency on the one hand ("Come unto me all ye that labor and are heavy laden") and progressive independence on the other ("You shall have power to do greater things than these because I go to the Father").

The Question of Isolation

There is a second aspect of the authority/dependency conflict that applies to the question of isolation. The comfortable dependency we find in Christ is not universally experienced in human relationships. Some of you grew up knowing only an insufficient authority figure whom you could never depend upon, or else one who overwhelmed you. Consequently, you prefer loneliness and isolation to admitting your dependency.

There was a bitter young father who felt he had been given a raw deal in life. He wanted to teach his four-year-old son how to survive in the cold, cruel world, so he took the lad out to the front porch. Standing below on the lawn, he said, "Jump to daddy!" The tot squealed and leaped into space only to have the waiting arms withdraw. He hit the ground with a thud, then was picked up, comforted, and placed on the porch again. "Now, daddy will catch you this time. Come on now. Jump to daddy." Again and again this happened. Finally the child choked out through his tears, "Why don't you catch me, daddy?" His father replied, "Well, son, I'm trying to teach you that you can't trust anybody!"

You Can't Trust Anybody!

This illustration is extreme, but that is the net experience of many children. They hear hollow promises of caring and relationship, only to be disappointed time after time. The lesson is learned: it hurts to be dropped, and it is better to avoid risking the injury that comes when you depend on others—"you can't trust anybody."

The discomfort produced by these wounds persists on a deep and often unconscious level. You very consciously realize that your authority could suffer from overexposure, and may justify your isolation on the basis of the need to maintain that authority. At the same time, you may completely deny your unreasonable avoidance of dependency. This in turn contributes heavily to your isolation and probably carries over even into your marriage and family relationships.

Max Stratton of the Fellowship of Christian Athletes' staff was recently reporting on a self-awareness group experience. The area of his personality brought forcefully and forcibly into his consciousness was his refusal to accept help from the group. He was a gracious helper but he felt unrealistically uncomfortable in the position of need.

The Dread of Dependency

The anxiety produced by the unconscious dread of dependency and by the reawakening of those childhood hurts may never surface if the security of being the healer is never threatened. Most of us will not live life immune from those crisis times when our own dependency becomes painfully apparent. Times when these crises most probably occur are: sickness, death of a loved one, or failure in some significant area of life, such as loss of a job.

The common denominator in each of these events is the threat to the integrity of "self." Incapacitated by physical illness, we are forced to depend on care from others. In grief, we are faced with loneliness and loss that brutally reminds us of our interdependence and the risk of separation. Life's failures throw a glaring searchlight on our inadequacy, focusing our attention on our inability to do everything single-handedly. All of these situations may be coped with in relative comfort if one has had his early dependency needs adequately met, for then he knows he will not be insulted, diminished, or destroyed by admitting his weakness. But that's not true of everyone. To those of you who have been sensitized to dependency by repeated rejection at times of need, isolation appears safer than risking closeness. The isolation may be expressed by your fear of allowing friendships to develop. You may avoid revealing yourself to colleagues, congregation, or even to your spouse.

I met John a year or so ago. A good example of such isolation, he is a middle-aged pastor who described himself as having been a loner all his life. His wife agreed that he allowed no one to know him intimately, including her. Presenting himself as a self-reliant perfectionist, an image designed to intimidate everyone he met, he confessed that inside he was scared and insecure, but afraid to let anyone know it. He was terrified that they might not accept him if he wasn't perfect. In childhood he was never accepted unless he did everything without error. He grew up hiding his doubts behind a façade of intellectualism and achievement, and avoiding detection by isolation. For John, the moment of truth came as his marriage relationship began to deteriorate. He then realized he had given little to the marriage and didn't really know how to begin. Suddenly unable to hide from the discomfort he faced in all his relationships, he discovered that he wanted to feel close to people, especially his wife.

As John was willing to risk exposing his fears to me, his wife, and our therapy group, he began to feel acceptance for the imperfect, scared self which he had been concealing from others all his life. Furthermore, he became sensitive to those fears in others whom he had always assumed really were secure in themselves. What a relief to see the truth for the first time and find a common ground for sharing life—our frail humanity.

11

Unexpressed Hostility

A second common conflict for the clergyman is that of unexpressed hostility. Actually, this is an inaccurate term, because anger usually finds expression in some form and toward some target. Better stated then, the problem is with hostility inappropriately handled.

Ministers deal with people, and people (even the Christian variety) can be frustrating. The local butcher can tell off an annoying old busybody. Not so the man of God. You must smile and take what comes. What happens to that black urge to let her have a piece of your mind? Basically two things. Either it is expressed directly—verbally or physically—or it is denied and excluded from consciousness. The former method seems unworkable, so the denial mechanism is brought into play.

Repression

The technique of repression is never permanently effective. The feelings driven into the unconscious always seep out. (It's like my attempts to save steps. I hate to make extra trips to do any task; so I am frequently seen making a mad dash somewhere with both hands full, articles stuffed under each elbow, balanced on my forearms, slipping from beneath my chin, clenched tightly in my teeth, and wobbling precariously between my knees. Then that one last item I want comes into view. Invariably I try to tuck it under, stack it up on, or stuff it into some appendage only to lose two more bits of baggage from the other side.) That is the way it is with anger and the unconscious. It just keeps popping out somewhere else, *often even in Sunday's sermons.* (Ever hear a scathing delivery of righteous condemnation that somehow seemed a mite over-zealous? Ever preach one?) Or perhaps the anger leaks out at your wife or family.

Depression

Not infrequently, the only expression of anger is that deflected toward self, and an overwhelming depression descends. I'll never forget a minister from the west coast who was deeply depressed. He felt guilty for all his sinfulness, miserable about his failures, sad and tearful over lost opportunities, and blamed himself for it all. He had trouble sleeping, felt weak and fatigued, and he had lost weight. In fact he was a wreck. We explored his life history and initially heard only joyful and happy tales of an idyllic childhood. After several hours of counseling, the memories, which had been repressed and unconscious, painfully began to return. At first he still denied feeling any anger or resentment toward those who had mistreated him, continuing to heap on himself all the anger. He vividly described how his father would beat him frequently with a six-foot bull whip until he bled. Such punishment would come for insignificant misbehavior or without reason, yet the anger generated by this brutality had been carefully concealed and redirected toward himself. Initially the brutality was recounted unemotionally, but the repressed anger finally emerged. After it was identified and verbally released, with a great deal of emotion, he could like himself and even forgive his father. Then the depression lifted.

Anger toward God

There are times when one feels anger toward God, as well as the flock. Frank is a middle-aged pastor who entered the ministry late in life. He had been a skilled technician and competent in his field. Now, after about five years in full-time service for the Lord, he looked back over some difficult and at times desperate struggles. More than once he wanted to throw in the towel and go back to his former work. He blamed his parishioners, his wife, his children, Satan, and himself for the misery. At times he even wondered what God had in mind to put him through the pain. His anger has been thoroughly expressed toward his flock, his wife, his children, Satan, and himself—but never toward God.

I have come to discover that God is big enough to accept my fury, and I have even felt furious at him several times. Jeremiah was able to face God honestly with his rage. Elijah openly expressed his weariness and discouragement. David felt a freedom to talk about his anger toward God. I wonder if Christ's agonizing, "My God, why have you forsaken me?" did not contain an element of anger, bitterness, and resentment. Christ must have known these feelings in connection with being forsaken. It hurts to be forsaken. Furthermore, he expressed them honestly both toward his Father and toward Peter, James, and John, who were unable to wait while he prayed.

What does unexpressed hostility have to do with the authority-dependency relationship? If one experiences comfortable acceptance and forgiveness in his early dependency relationships, he has freedom to express negative emotions without fear of rejection or reprisal. In fact, getting the anger out into the open usually opens the door to a closer, more secure relationship.

There are times when I make mistakes as a parent. In particular, I often forget something I promised to do. On such occasions my children have just cause for resentment. At other times my decision simply disagrees with their desires and their resultant disappointment becomes expressed as anger. I have attempted to accept that anger and at times even help them identify those feelings. I hope they are discovering that our love relationship is strong enough to survive the anger inevitable between us as human beings. As a by-product, they are learning to forgive and receive forgiveness, to accept another individual's anger, and to enjoy the warmth of reconciliation.

Mastering the Problem

But what if the lesson of expressing negative feelings toward an authority figure, without fear of rejection, has been missed in childhood? It may still be learned. With work you can ultimately find honest sharing much more comfortable and non-threatening. This is especially beneficial for you and your congregation, since in some respects this relationship repeats the dependency status for you. The nature of this relationship should be explored and perhaps clarified. How do you feel about your dependency on your people? If you are frightened by the prospect of sharing anger directly, because of dependence on the congregation, the relationship may never develop into one of depth and honesty.

Though you are financially and emotionally dependent on your people, your primary dependence should rest on God, in whom ultimate authority resides. I have known several ministers who have verbalized to their parishioners that they are working primarily for God. This honest understanding has helped to remove the dread of conflict. At times, however, even to settle the authority-dependency question between the minister and his flock does not remove the dread of expressing negative feelings. There still arises considerable anxiety over the prospect of openly facing a conflict with those whom we love. At these times you must look into your own background to discover what early negative experiences with authority were endured and what effect those hurts now have.

12

Failure and Inadequacy

I haven't received an award for several years. No convention has recognized my efforts. The mayor has not yet proclaimed Louis McBurney Day. Fortunately, however, the Lord blessed me with a sensitive wife who consistently commends me for all my efforts and unashamedly shares her conviction that I am super. I eat it up. It keeps me going to get her praise. Although I don't think I am particularly self-centered, a significant part of my God-given male ego is the need to feel effective and adequate. At times this is hard to achieve in a pastorate, where expectations are unrealistic, goals ill-defined, and a solid measure of achievement lacking.

Tom's Problem

Before he left the ministry, Tom had been widely acclaimed during his twenty years of service as a tireless, effective, missionary-minded go-getter. Each church he served grew dramatically in numbers and enthusiasm. Missions and preaching points soon dotted the area. In counseling after his resignation, however, Tom revealed a lifelong history of self-doubt and an inescapable sense of failure. He had never been able to do enough and be acclaimed sufficiently to overcome the gnawing inner ache of inadequacy.

Just before he came into therapy a friend had asked him, "What's driving you, man?" We discovered what was driving Tom. It was his inability to please his tyrannical father, whose expectations for his son made no provisions for serving God. Tom had spent his life trying to do enough to merit his father's approval. To make matters worse, his obsessive work habits demanded the abandonment of his wife. She was embittered by this neglect and began to aim her resentment at his weakest point, his self-image. She could deftly disarm and destroy him by her biting criticism in the presence of their friends. His only means of combat was to avoid her and work harder.

Tom's problems derived primarily from his demoralizing exposures to a despotic authority figure, whom he could never hope to please. It is not at all uncommon, as the emerging youth overthrows the tyranny of such a dictatorship, that fulfilment is sought in the service of others, in a sense attempting to atone for the sins of the father, as well as trying to finally become "good" enough. The failure and inadequacy which many ministers feel may have been derived originally from their relationships to early authority figures.

Then, on the other end of the scale, the same sense of inadequacy is generated by the *overprotective* parent. There may be encouragement and verbal approval, but the non-verbal message is always there: "Here, let me help you," with its implications, "You are not capable of performing without my supervision." It is difficult for such children ever to cut the cord and comfortably stand alone. If they finally succeed in leaving home, the deep-seated self-image of inadequacy goes with them, demanding continuous recognition and reassurance.

The Pastor with the Father Figure

A few years ago I was consulted by members of the board of elders of an urban church. They had recently hired a new pastor after their former minister retired. The replacement had come highly recommended from a small but growing church. They had not considered it unusual that he had insisted on bringing his assistant pastor. The assistant was an older man nearing retirement age. In a short time the group noticed that he was like a father to their pastor.

The problem they were now concerned about was the pastor's total reliance on his "father-assistant." He was unable to make any decisions without first getting approval. They justifiably questioned whether he would be able to serve them effectively after his assistant had retired.

In a sharing session during a church leadership retreat, the minister was able to reveal the story of his childhood. He was the only child of middle-aged parents, the long-awaited answer to their prayers for a baby. Understandably protective, they adored and doted on him, granting his slightest wish. However, they not only spoiled him with gifts and attention, but they also supervised his every move. He emerged from this smothering childhood with little self-reliance and a paralyzing feeling of inadequacy. Since his parents' death, which he miraculously survived, he had sought a succession of surrogate parents to reassure and encourage him.

I began this chapter by pointing out the basic need for praise. Now I have come to the point of illustrating how overindulgence of this need may indicate a deep-seated sense of inadequacy. If the craving for more and more applause intrudes into your character and behavior, we must ask with Tom's friend, "What's driving you, man?" The answer will often lie in an unquenchable thirst for approval, arising either from the wounds of rejection or the choking cloak of over-protection.

13

Job Insecurity

A fourth gnawing threat to the minister's peace of mind is that of losing his job. Not many of you have tenure. Although pastors' contracts vary greatly from denomination to denomination, with some of you enjoying significantly more security than others, even when you are assured of being "employed" it remains of utmost importance to your self-esteem to feel effective and accepted. Being asked to resign may be a welcome relief from some chaotic church situations, but it hurts deeply nonetheless. Obviously, all the problems of personality which we have already discussed contribute to job insecurity.

Another factor is the peculiar employer-employee relationship that characterizes the ministry. There are few positions for which an employee is paid, in part, for telling his employers (the congregation) what they are doing wrong. That is the usual perception of the preacher's position, although this concept is inaccurate. The man of God is just that—God's man —not the man employed by the First Church. It may seem to you impossible to convince the board of deacons that their pastor takes orders from God, but I have known several preachers who have done just that and lived to tell about it!

Within the fabric of the more traditional church/pastor relationship, authority and dependency are the warp and woof of a tapestry beset by flaws. Even when the authority supposedly rests solidly on the Scriptures, there can develop an uncomfortable interdependence between you and your people that does not wear well. The confrontation is expressed: "Who is in authority here?" Frequently the anxiety builds to a critical point and explosion is unavoidable. You are thoroughly aware of this threat and may have avoided it by frequent moves before the boiling point is reached. This maneuver contributes to an amazing statistic: the average length of a pastorate is just over two years! It is significant to note that when a new pastor arrives in a church he is realistically dependent on the knowledge and leadership of the people. When he is able to establish himself and has become acquainted with the congregation, his own need to control becomes more important. The honeymoon ends as his dependency tapers off and he begins taking over the reins.

With frightening regularity the battle for control repeats itself. Of course, it is not solely the minister's need to exert his authority that precipitates conflict. In every congregation there are usually people who have never learned to submit themselves to those in authority over them. Let's face it, most of us aren't too good at following directions. If our limbs were as unwieldy as the various parts of the spiritual body, we'd be cripples. Our head would say, "Okay, hands, get some food up to the mouth," and they'd probably stick it in our ears!

By the same token the head needs to be sensitive to the body parts. For instance, if I get a rock in my shoe, my foot signals my head that something is wrong, "Hey, up there! There's a rock in our shoe and it hurts like crazy!"

"That's okay. We've got a long way to go. We can't stop now. You just be quiet and cooperate. I know what I'm doing!"

"I realize you're in control here, but you haven't done as much walking as I have, and this really isn't very comfortable. I don't think we ought to go on."

"Now, look, I've got the big picture and have a better grasp on the total objectives than you do way down there. Just trust and obey—and keep moving!"

Now if my head is that insensitive to my foot's problems, we'll all have such a severe stone bruise we'll be crippled up for days.

Fortunately, my body parts don't get into squabbles about who is in authority and go shuffling about from body to body, trying to find a place to exert control. His body, the church, should offer the same job security.

14

Role Confusion

Referring to John the Baptist, Christ said, "What went ye out into the wilderness to see? A reed shaken by the wind? A man clothed in soft raiment? . . . But what went ye out to see? A prophet? Yea, I say unto you, and more than a prophet" (Matt. 11:7–9).

I wonder what Christ would say today about the man of God? Carlyle Marney describes the dichotomy of roles expected of the minister in terms of priest and prophet. Frequently in the priestly function you are reduced to becoming the preserver of the culture and tradition. The prophetic role of interpreter of God to the current generation is often watered down or lost altogether.

Within these two broad roles is found a clutter of tasks usually thrust upon your shoulders: theologian, counselor, teacher, administrator, janitor, financial advisor, fund raiser, and welfare dispenser, not to mention husband and father. It's not at all amazing that confusion and a perpetual identity crisis should pervade your career. Complicating these traditional expectations is the drastic culture change of attitude evidenced in the last fifteen years. Rather than polite respect for your profession, you may confront frank criticism and hostility.

For the purpose of discussion let me simplify this astonishingly complex issue by ignoring the last factor of cultural change. Let us rather focus on the two roles of priest and prophet, and how authority and dependency differ between them.

I have observed that most ministers are most comfortable and least confused as priest. Here you represent the people before God through our cherished sacraments. You add beauty and a sacred mystery to our lives through administering communion. This awesome and soul-searching experience humbles us and reminds us of our dependency on God the Father, and the atoning work of Christ. You baptize us into fellowship within the church, standing as representative not only of God but of the church as the body of Christ.

Likewise, in *The Common Ventures of Life*, Elton Trueblood observes, even the most non-religious among us will frequently seek to solemnize and sanctify marriage by enlisting a "priest" to perform the ceremony.

Finally, it is your priestly function to commit us to our Creator and comfort the bereaved. Herein you move with dignity, grace, and *authority*. Herein we come as little children admitting our *dependence* upon the Father and on you as his representative. The relationship is clear-cut and unquestioned.

Have you ever heard an irate and pompous pillar of the church indignantly challenge, "Who does he think he is, baptizing in the name of the Father, the Son and the Holy Spirit?" Can you imagine a fussy matron moaning, "From dust to dust—well the nerve!"?

Now change your priestly robes for prophetic, lay aside ceremony, and take up the Word. Put away condolences and issue challenge. Trade tradition and trappings for "thus saith the Lord." Question our values and disrupt our comfortable prejudices. We respond by transforming childlike humility to defensive autonomy. Are we not capable of interpreting God's Word as well as you? Aren't you our hired servant? You must have forgotten that generous gift I gave last year! In your role as prophet you have reminded us of our dependency at a time that we don't welcome it. You have assumed authority in its chastening aspect, and remind us that Jesus is not only Savior but Lord.

Throughout history the spokesmen of God have paid with their lives. Jesus said, "O Jerusalem, Jerusalem, thou that killest the prophets, and stonest them which are sent unto thee" (Matt. 23:37). Jerusalem is still stoning prophets. As today's prophet you often pay by sacrificing a vital part of life —your identity. You become the "reed shaken by the wind" and one "dressed in fine raiment," but confused, bewildered, and frustrated.

Part IV

The Imprisoned

Turning to the Jews who had believed him, Jesus said, "If you dwell within the revelation I have brought, you are indeed my disciples; you shall know the truth and the truth will set you free" (John 8:31 NEB).

When we were teen-agers, we would spend Sunday afternoon conducting a service at the old county jail. I carried a red Bible and wore a smile, but inside I was scared to death. We could feel the loneliness and isolation of the inmates and knew that those heavy iron bars were only an outward symbol of an inward captivity. We sensed that they might never be really free. I never knew whether our songs and testimonies penetrated those defensive walls to bring freedom, but I will never forget my first exposure to men locked away.

I have come to see ministers as being similarly imprisoned. Some of the bars are erected by society; others, just as real, are built by the ministers themselves. These walls built for protection become a prison keeping pastors from seeking help for their emotional hurts.

My most frustrating experience as a psychiatrist has been seeing men and women in pain who are unwilling to accept the freedom available to them. Although their defensive position seems to be their safest alternative, the truth they are afraid to face—about themselves—truly has the capacity to liberate them, just as Jesus has the power to set us free from sin's imprisonment. Instead, they choose to cower behind their protective barriers. What are these barriers and why do they persist?

15

The Pedestal Barrier (The Parishioner's Viewpoint)

The most widely recognized of these barriers is the pedestal. Any of you can tell how it feels to be put on a pedestal. Most will admit that it is a bit dizzying up there, and that a fear of height sets in. Some will confess that it is not all bad and in fact feels pretty good at times. A few of you are aware of your own role in maintaining the height advantage. I am sure all will agree that when you are deified it becomes increasingly difficult to say, "Wait a minute. I'm human. I have problems I can't seem to cope with, and I need help!"

Why the Pedestal

Why the pedestal in the first place? We all know intellectually that our ministers are human beings, and not God. From the perspective of the people, the semi-deification attempts to serve several purposes: our need for an omnipotent, benevolent father; an expression of the all-American trait of hero worship; the desire for a personal high priest; and the all-too-frequent practice of commitment to Christ by proxy. Let's look at each one.

Sometime during adolescence most of us come to that awful discovery that our parents are not all-powerful and all-knowing. Many never fully recover, and they spend the rest of their lives looking for the perfect parent who seemed to disappear when he was needed most. The adolescent quickly finds an idealized substitute: a teacher, a coach, an interested young adult, or the parent of a friend. These serve nicely for a few years, but as the enthusiasm and idealism of youth give way to adult realism and responsibilities, fewer parent figures remain available.

Often the last to go—if ever relinquished—is the pastor.

To have someone to lean on whom we see as always dependable offers us great security. When doubt bombards us and our faith is shaken, there is little consolation in an uncertain counselor. To combat fear we crave the fearless; to bind our wounds, the healer; to reassure, the confident. We expect you pastors to be all these things. The weak, frightened child in us wants so desperately to maintain the myth, "Here is my perfect father." Periodically, when you fail to live up to these expectations, we trade off the tarnished image for a shiny new model, whitewash the pedestal, and perpetuate the myth. Then you can go fulfill some other church's high hopes.

We lived in London for a year and were impressed by the differences in cultures between England and the United States, though they are alike in many ways. Ours is an action-oriented life style steeped with the tradition of Yankee ingenuity. Our British cousins are frustratingly more cautious and deliberate. Where we act, they discuss. At our weekly hospital staff meetings, I became increasingly irritated by the avoidance of taking action on anything. After I considered myself no longer a newcomer (in about four months) I impetuously, and in a characteristically American style, offered the observation that no decisions were ever made, no action taken. I was told that after all it is more important to thoroughly discuss an issue than "to take a decision."

One side effect of our preference for action is a great affinity for heroes. Nowhere in Europe did I see quite the zeal for the superstar that we display in the United States. There, much more caution is used in "buying" an opinion and the gullibility for "the expert" was joyfully absent. The all-American arouses our patriotic image of the American dream and gives us at least a vicarious share in its fulfilment. As minister-hero, you can fill the bill, and the more sensational, spectacular, and supercolossal we parishioners can convince ourselves you are, the better it is for our own sagging egos. What's really super is that we can be on a first name basis with our all-American pulpiteer. I'm not saying we shouldn't be proud of you ministers, but often we fail to keep the balance between admiration and idolatry. You end up—way up —on the pedestal.

The Pastor As a High Priest

We've looked at the pedestal for a perfect parent and personal hero. What about for high priest? One legitimate role you serve is that of priest. You baptize us, marry us, bury us, give us communion, and hear our confessions. Whether these functions are performed with more or less ritual is insignificant for our discussion. We still feel the need for a human representative of God to perform these highly meaningful ceremonies. What's more, the more excellent our priest, the more fulfilling the event. Thus we may call a former pastor or prominent minister to conduct a wedding or funeral. Similarly, popular, dynamic preachers are often sought as confessors by persons outside their parish. The higher the pedestal, the higher the priest, and the more impressive the priestly function, the more status and glory to be shared by the participants. To be ministered to by the bishop is better than by the parish priest. And if we rate an archbishop, better yet!

There are times, of course, when this whole system may backfire. I know of a prominent young pastor who has become so popular and in such demand as a conference speaker that his services to his own church have suffered significantly. Initially, this notoriety was a source of tremendous pride for his home church. The glow of his success has begun to fade, however, and what is felt at home now are the congregation's unmet needs. His status as a spiritual superstar has finally created a crisis in his own job responsibilities. Those who fanned the flames of his popularity are now eager to extinguish the blaze.

Finally, we laymen build pedestals to capture and control a sort of spiritual gigolo, a substitute saint whom we can pay off to be perfect. We are content to allow our commitment to extend only to providing your wages. You are then our paid representative to pray, read the Word, witness, minister to those in need, and do any other Christian duty we don't enjoy. Furthermore, this is all done at the bargain rate of about $1.75 an hour! Not a bad deal at that. Perhaps this is a reflection of our propensity for spectator sports. We hire performers in every area of life.

Whatever the cause, we repeatedly set you pastors up, often in a precarious position. You must be aware of our propensity to do that to you and you'd be wise to avoid it, especially since there are desires inside you that will make it very tempting! Let's look at those now.

16

The Pedestal Barrier (The Minister's Perspective)

From the minister's viewpoint the pedestal is appealing in several ways. It feels good. There is a nice safe buffer zone between him and his people, and he can avoid facing his own frustrations and failures.

A minister who had served various churches for seventeen years was recently sharing tales of his early pastorates. The worst year he could recall was his first out of seminary. One could feel the anguish of it as he told of ninety-hour weeks, never seeing his family, and being used by the people. Why did he do such a thing? They were constantly offering him the pedestal: "My, you're better than Pastor Smith who just left." It did feel good, just out of seminary and wet behind the ears, to be so adored.

The Pedestal of Praise

I would be far less than honest if I did not readily admit my own pleasure in receiving praise. We all have a need to be accepted, and to be acclaimed is a bonus. And we must learn to be gracious receivers of man's praise. I don't know anything that turns people off more than to have their gift of praise belittled or refused. How do you feel when you say to your wife, "Sweetheart, you sure look beautiful," and she says, "Oh, no, I don't, I look awful"? Ever want to just quit giving her compliments? Well, that's how people feel when you refuse to accept their praise, but always say, "It wasn't me; it was the Lord." The danger rests in believing that only "self" is worthy of the worship and failing to share the glory with the Lord. If God created us, sustains us, and enables us to achieve, then it is logical that he would desire our success and fulfilment, just as we share the warm glow of praise that comes to our children. The joy over our offspring's success cools only if they reject and disclaim our parentage. Our relationship to the Lord is the same. It gives him great pleasure and joy for us to achieve a measure of success, for in so doing we are bringing praise to him. Unless, that is, we forget that he is responsible.

The Pedestal Provides Distance

A second ministerial motivation for maintaining the lofty position atop the pedestal is the comfortable distance to the commoners below. There has been the general belief in psychiatry that one must avoid closeness on a personal or social level with his patients. Without a doubt the therapeutic relationship may be endangered by too close an involvement. However, many therapists are finding that some social contacts may be permitted without undermining the beneficial aspects of the doctor-patient interaction. The greatest threat that comes from too much closeness is a loss of objectivity on the part of the therapist. But our fear has been that if the truth were known that the doctor is human, too, there could be little reliance on this mere mortal.

A similar system (though intensified) surrounds your relationship with your congregation. You sense their need for a hero and an unblemished priest, and are afraid of complete rejection if the hard fact of your humanity is revealed. Furthermore, in your case, the added dimension of moral perfection enters the picture. The psychiatrist can escape with his reputation and professional image, should he have some moral failings. You have no such latitude for error. Thus the distance is welcomed. The admonition, "Let him who is without sin cast the first stone," has long since lost any application when the sinner is ordained. Furthermore, the question of "what is sin?" comes to be determined by any and every member of the congregation. It is no wonder that most of you prefer to keep a certain comfortable distance between yourself and your people. So you welcome the pedestal.

The Pedestal As an Opiate

Finally, the pedestal offers itself as an opiate for the pains of failure and frustrations you face as a clergyman. One of the critical issues confronting you is that of being unable to meet the expectations placed on you. You are expected to be the all-American supersaint for whom the pedestal was designed. Few men can live up to that advance billing. When you, who believe the rave notices, come to look at yourselves honestly, an overwhelming sense of failure soon stares you in the face. An alternative to that devastating experience is to accept the pedestal and perhaps even begin blindly to accept the "hero" inscriptions. From that more comfortable stance it is easy to blame all problems on "them" and quit looking at yourself at all. At Marble Retreat, we've had three different ministers in the past year who have been asked to resign their pastorates for various reasons. All three have clung to their own pedestal image and pointed an accusing finger at their deacons or elders, their associate staff, or their wives and family. In all three instances, significant problems in their own personalities and ability to relate contributed to the crisis, but were steadfastly denied. The pedestal is a sticky and persistent barrier to admitting the need for help or allowing anyone else to come to your aid.

17

The Personality Barrier

Not only does the pedestal create an obstacle to your getting help, but basic personality traits often enter in. I've frequently compared the minister to the physician. Here again a striking similarity is seen. Both are in helping roles and are far more comfortable being the helper than the helped. Our own dependency needs are most comfortably dealt with by denial. We say, "I simply don't have any needs. I am omnipotent and self-sufficient."

This basic characteristic leads to such behaviors as fast driving and refusal to look after one's physical health (I am indestructible). My friend, Greg Livingston, is a pastor in Aspen, Colorado. Greg says if he were an artist he would draw a cartoon picturing his guardian angel crouched fearfully on his car fender warding off other automobiles as he drives down the road with his mind miles away. With a terrified expression the angel would be looking upward and pleading, "Please, Lord, couldn't I have another assignment?"

The Pastor and His Mask

You sincerely and conscientiously counsel your parishioners to drive safely and take care of themselves medically, but you fail to practice what you preach. You seem to believe that to do so is to admit to imperfection and dependency. These feelings are intensified when we move from the physical into the emotional realm. To be unable to cope with anxiety, fear, depression, loneliness, or anger seems childish. We don't even want to come to God as little children, much less to a psychiatrist. In psychotherapy groups at the Mayo Clinic, we consistently observed the reluctance of ministers to unmask and admit their problems. Their defensiveness was noticeably more tenacious than that of non-ministers.

Another aspect of personality that may be important is the minister's sexual identification and self-image as a male. It has long been observed that clergymen tend to reflect more traditionally feminine interests on psychological profiles. This does not necessarily indicate an abnormal sexual identification, but rather a higher sensitivity to feelings, more appreciation of the arts and literature, and a more comfortable participation in household activities. Needless to say, these are valuable assets. A man who is secure regarding his maleness finds such attributes and activities non-threatening. A broader experience of living is available through such activities.

However, there are many clergymen who do harbor serious doubts about their masculinity. Often a significant female has encouraged their entry into the ministry, and they have never felt wholehearted masculine approval. Their duties carry them primarily into a female–dominated subculture—today's church —limiting their involvement with men and masculine activities. This environment may intensify underlying doubts and fears. Given these self-doubts and assuming that psychiatrists are obsessed with sex, it is not surprising that consulting a psychiatrist would be avoided. Such exposure is threatening to most people, and it can appear devastating to the man of God, especially if his masculine self-image is sagging.

The Pastor and His Personality

Besides a denial of dependency and some sexual identity problems, some ministers have a basically rigid, moralistic personality marked by inflexibility and narrow-mindedness. Such a personality may develop to control underlying doubts or unacceptable impulses. These unconscious (or at times even conscious) passions are kindled by exposure to society's expressions of that drive. For instance, if I have to battle an inner impulse to eat cherry pie, which is not allowed by my conscience, I become terribly anxious if my neighbor throws a big cherry pie party. I either attack him viciously or avoid him assiduously.

Similarly, a rigid individual may withdraw from the world to escape the "cherry pie" anxiety. It is hard to relate effectively to the world one seeks to reach for Christ when entrenched in this way. Consequently, the conflicts are unavoidable and may precipitate painful anxiety or rage. The need for help may be critical and the discomfort unbearable. Yet equally threatening is the thought of consulting a psychiatrist or even a colleague. This might involve looking squarely into the face of the doubt and the urge to eat cherry pie.

Ed was a righteous, legalistic preacher who exposed sin whenever he suspected it. This was usually in the area of sexual promiscuity and impurity. Behind his mask of piety and zealous moralism, he struggled with unspeakable sexual urges and fantasies. These impulses heightened his fear and avoidance of sex. Then he had occasion to travel alone to a strange city where he was unknown. By chance he found himself on a street lined with pornographic book stores. He gave in to his strong sexual drive and curiosity and watched an "adult movie." He was instantly overcome with anxiety and guilt that was incapacitating. After a period of psychiatric treatment that included medication for his uncontrolled anxiety, he was able to face his sexual fears and fantasies, to understand their origin in his childhood, to accept his sexuality as being God-given, and ultimately to return to an effective ministry. He didn't become an immoral person, but like his Master, he could associate with sinners without anxiety and with forgiveness.

I think there is an unfortunate conspiracy against you ministers that prevents you from getting help for some of these personality problems that have plagued you all your lives. The traits themselves are in league with your professional image.

18

The Theology Barrier

A prevalent attitude among both parishioner and preacher in some denominations is that an ordained minister who is in right relationship to God should never have to turn to a psychiatrist for help. Doesn't the Lord promise to give us strength for bearing our burdens? Doesn't the Word promise healing through prayer? Isn't "self" at the root of all personality problems? Thus, when desperation disrupts prayer life, and God begins to seem distant and disinterested, the minister begins to feel guilty that he is unable to claim the victory and peace he proclaims. The most frequent defense is denial—often until a breaking point is reached. That may be too late for effective help.

I embrace those same scriptural promises and claim them often through the ministry of other human beings. As I understand New Testament theology, God is represented not only by the indwelling Holy Spirit but also by the members of his body, the church. We are to minister to each other's needs as part of his body. That body even includes a few psychiatrists!

The Pastor and Psychiatry

A few years ago a major denominational group in Texas conducted a survey of psychological needs among their ministers. The results demonstrated that a significant number at one time or another had felt the desire for psychiatric support. In response to these data, a counseling service for ministers was proposed. This suggestion ignited an explosion of protests from throughout the state. Letter after letter came from individuals who felt strongly that there was no place within the denomination for ministers who needed psychiatric counseling.

I would venture to guess that people in this same group would not hesitate to see a physician for a medical problem. Nor would they have any hesitation in sending a fellow Christian for counseling to a minister or otherwise qualified counselor. Why then should you ministers be singled out and expected never to suffer the same emotional stress that the rest of us feel? The truth is that when you are hurting and at the end of your rope, you may be unable to vault this theological wall between you and the helping professional.

It is not at all unusual for some Christians to question my call as a psychiatrist for ministers. They seem to take one of two positions. Either they naively refuse to believe that Christian ministers can have emotional problems, or they cannot understand why prayer does not bring instant healing.

The answer to both questions is the same: the unconscious forces in our lives are more controlling and difficult to understand than most people realize. Patterns of behavior and ways of dealing with feelings are well established quite early in development. Painful childhood experiences that have been forced into the unconscious, influence our relationships moment by moment. And when the integrity of the self is threatened, anxiety, hostility, depression, physical symptoms, and even insanity may result.

God still works out the healing of the mind. He may work through a minister, through silent meditation, through the loving support of community, through a psychiatrist, or more probably, through all these avenues of healing.

19

The Psychiatric Barrier

One other barrier deserves comment—the psychiatric. The professional reputation we bear represents a real barrier to many clergymen and Christians. We are seen as a godless group who preach a gospel of "do your own thing," "outgrow your childish notions of a heavenly Father," and "what you need to do is broaden your sexual experiences and all will be well." I cannot deny that such concepts have been offered by some psychotherapists. However, I have not personally known these individuals, and I have found that most of my colleagues recognize the integrative function of religious practice and belief. During therapy, religious strengths are not only allowed to remain but are encouraged by the sensitive psychotherapist.

Some legitimate questions to ask are: Can a non-Christian psychiatrist deal effectively with my problems as a minister? Can he possibly understand? Will he offer therapy that will be compatible with my theological beliefs and my moral convictions?

Let me address these questions first by sharing a surprising discovery. I have found that among the ministers whom I have counseled, vocational or theological issues have been relatively infrequent as primary causes of their problems. Instead, most have come with basic personality difficulties related to early life experiences that were brought along into the ministry. It is true, however, that the particular stresses of the calling have in some instances intensified a conflict which otherwise might have remained undisturbed.

For this reason I must conclude that a special knowledge of theology or the vocational pressures is not absolutely necessary for a psychiatrist to be helpful. Most competently trained psychiatrists (or clinical psychologists) can effectively identify the unconscious elements that are significant and assist you in "working through" the areas of conflict. Many of the techniques used, such as medical treatment, individual psychotherapy, group interaction, marital and family counseling, and behavior modification, may be successfully employed regardless of the religious beliefs of the therapist.

There are, however, some psychological theories and individual practitioners incompatible with basic Christian doctrine. For this reason it is important to see what you are getting into before you sign up.

You should know that there is a rapidly expanding network of Christian counseling centers, some specializing in the problems of ministers. A recent issue of *Search* *, a journal for ministers, carries an excellent article titled "Where to Go for Help" by Dr. James Cooper. The article points out that most denominations have some structure provided for counseling its ministers. If the denominational framework is too threatening, as it sometimes seems to be, one can seek advice from local professionals or take advantage of private interdenominational centers such as Interpreters' House, Marble Retreat, and others. If a local private psychiatrist is to be consulted, his orientation and attitudes can usually be discovered by asking members of the medical community or the psychiatrist himself.

If you who are suffering from emotional problems are to know the truth and become free, you must recognize and overcome the private barriers that imprison you. Perhaps you have done this as you were reading these pages. Don't continue to let the walls remain.

---

* James L. Cooper, "Where to Go for Help," *Search*, Vol. 5, No. 4 (1975), p. 45.

Part V

Out of Bondage

Pharaoh was almost upon them when the Israelites looked up and saw the Egyptians close behind. In their terror they clamoured to the Lord for help and said to Moses, "Were there no graves in Egypt that you should have brought us here to die in the wilderness?" (Exod. 14:10, 11 NEB).

Did you ever feel that God had released you from bondage to sin only to leave you to die in the wilderness of the ministry? There are so many wanderers, men lost in a bewildering wasteland, no longer pilgrims on a journey, just bruised, confused, and hopeless strugglers. I've tried to describe the wilderness of unrealistic expectations, of problems, and of barriers to finding help. Now let's look ahead toward the promised land. How can you find the way?

Jesus told Nicodemus, "You must be born again." He tells each of us the same thing. One aspect of rebirth that we need is a newborn understanding of who we are. Ask yourself: Who am I, where am I going, and, importantly, do I love myself? To adequately and honestly answer these questions one must be in touch with his own feelings. Perhaps as you have been reading you have identified with some of the problems and conflicts. Before you quickly cover up the discomfort that emerges, allow those feelings to come to full awareness. Just as a newborn infant is suddenly confronted with a vast array of stimuli, and just as a newborn Christian becomes alive to spirituality, so must you allow your sensitivity to long–denied feelings to develop to maturity.

What feelings are there? A sense of failure and inadequacy plagues many ministers. Guilt feelings threaten others. Anger may burst into consciousness. Fear is often a prominent adversary. Depression darkens the pastor's existence from time to time. For one who has practiced hiding his feelings from others and from himself, even the strong, positive feelings of love, joy, and compassion may have to be rediscovered. There are many of you who are equally uncomfortable with any and all of your feelings, for you have been carefully taught to avoid them. For a change, let's look at them, dissect them, define them, but deny them no longer, because denied and locked in the unconscious, these feelings frequently interfere with interpersonal relationships and with real self-fulfilment and joy.

20

Recognizing Your Emotions

Failure and Insecurity

The extent of this problem is brought home to me every day. Nearby in the Aspen area a number of self-acceptance groups have developed. Transactional analysis groups, transcendental meditation and yoga classes, Erhardt Sensitivity Training (EST), countless strange occult conclaves, and Eastern religious sects—all advertise the same thing: peace of mind and a new sense of self-worth.

Bookstore shelves are lined with new volumes appealing to these same needs. Men and women look for fulfilment in sexual affairs, or they seek escape through alcoholism and drug abuse. Women's liberation seeks to provide answers for women who feel they have lost their individuality and self-worth.

Our original value system begins to be developed from the moment of birth, as we record the feelings transmitted to our waiting brain. The warmth and love, or the disappointment and rejection, begin to be stored in our unconscious. Through the years these impressions are intensified as countless memories accumulate. The outcome may be positive, and we enter adulthood with confidence and a feeling of success in living, or like many—perhaps most—of our fellow human beings, we step into adult responsibilities with insecurity about self and the expectation of failure.

Once established, this negative self-image and expectation of failure often perpetuate themselves. You may have said, "Everything I try is a disaster." Often it's no accident. You may set yourself up to fail, and you are relieved by this inevitable result. Let me tell you about a fellow who did just that.

Harvey is a pleasant, middle-aged minister who gives the initial impression of confidence and maturity. When he consulted me, he was beginning to be worried about the church where he had served as pastor for about eighteen months.

"This always happens," he confided. "I come to a new community. Everyone accepts me and the church begins to grow. Everything goes well for awhile, then it all falls apart."

As we explored the meanings of this situation, we discovered that as his work expands he begins to feel insecure about his ability to pastor so many and cope with their problems. He is uncomfortable with the praise and "success" and feels like a "phony." At that point his attention to his responsibilities begins to deteriorate. He becomes sensitive and irritable, and he starts to wait for the certain failure he has come to expect.

Harvey went on to share his memories of a childhood marked by rejection. Harvey's father had made it clear that he was an unwanted child and that he had forced the marriage that was a lifelong ordeal for both his parents. His father told him he could never do anything adequately, and very early in life Harvey began to consider himself a failure.

This image within created tension impossible for him to bear whenever he was faced with success. His avoidance of responsibilities, which were in reality well within his capabilities, assured failure and confirmed his lifelong negative image.

There are aspects peculiar to the ministry which contribute to the burden of insecurity and failure. One minister told me how thoroughly rewarding he found digging a ditch. If he had a ditch to dig, he first surveyed and marked off the outline. Then he began to work with pick and shovel. He would work up a sweat, gets calluses and blisters, and feel his back tiring out. The next day his muscles might ache as a constant reminder, but that didn't matter. There was the ditch. It was finished. No one could deny or question it, and he had done it with his own sore hands.

How unlike his pastoral duties which often have ill-defined

goals and uncertain end points. The nebulous nature of the ministry contributes to a sense of failure and inadequacy. To cement this firmly into the minister's self-image, all we need is the mortar of unrealistic expectations. We discussed these at length and described their genesis in childhood rejection and cultural desires for a perfect father. Confronted by this ideal, the minister often tries to be that father. He begins to believe that he actually can walk on water.

Speaking of walking on water, I heard a physician say recently, "I can do pretty well for about the first twenty yards; then I start to sink every time." As *you* sink, do you think, "Now, thank heavens I don't have to try to do that again!"? Or is your savior complex still punishing, "How could you let them down? You must try harder! Can't you do anything right?" I never cease to be amazed at the perfectionistic goals man will adopt (just short of walking on water), or the overriding sense of inadequacy felt when these goals predictably remain unrealized.

Guilt

In *A Psychiatrist Looks at Religion and Health*, James A. Knight clearly differentiates normal from neurotic guilt. It is the latter that controls some ministers. We effectively achieve forgiveness and a sense of atonement for real wrongdoing, but the guilt associated with imagined sin, for unconscious wishes, dogs us destructively.

Let me explain. The developing personality must assess and assimilate stimuli from without and from within. Among these are aggressive urges that arise from deep within all of us. Should these destructive drives, which are quite frightening to the child, occur at the same time some other threatening event happens, such as a feeling of rejection or the disintegration of the family, the ego may misinterpret the stimuli. What are actually unconnected events become linked in the unconscious. A three- or four-year-old may be aware of the wish to get daddy out of the way so he can have mother to himself. What he doesn't know is that his parents are unhappily married. So when daddy decides he'd rather live with his secretary, and divorces the family, the child's mind sees a cause-and-effect relationship between his desire to get rid of daddy and the divorce. The result is a deep-seated sense of guilt. The child-mind reasons, "My wish drove daddy away." Life may be spent in compulsive efforts to atone for a sin never actually committed.

This sort of guilt may be generated by the death of a parent or sibling, illness in the family, or financial failure. At times neurotic guilt may be thrust upon a child when anger and resentment of a parent who is trapped in some life crisis becomes deflected toward the child. The blame for the disaster is mercilessly placed on his head. The child is in no position to understand that he is in fact not guilty.

Gayle came to therapy after a long history of headaches. We discovered that she lived with overwhelming guilt regarding the death of a sister. Their mother had left the girls, ages three and five, alone while she went out with a friend for some drinks. There was a fire and only Gayle had been saved. Her little sister perished. Their mother was unable to cope with her own guilt over the tragedy and transferred it to her daughter. Gayle had relived that holocaust and the memory of her unsuccessful attempts to rescue her sister in recurrent nightmares for thirty years.

Now she was able for the first time to see the truth—it was not her fault. She had not been responsible. Her guilt and her headaches gradually subsided.

Anger

Of all the emotions in man's repertoire, anger is the most feared, avoided, abused, misdirected, and misunderstood. The Christian family seems particularly sensitized to anger and generally handles it poorly. The first attempt to avoid it is to change its name. I'll never forget a tense, depressed housewife in therapy at the Mayo Clinic. She was extremely hostile and often let fly a biting sarcasm. Her whole body showed the tension she felt: muscles tight, jaws clenched, eyes blazing with rage. When she was confronted by the group as appearing angry, she adamantly denied anything of the kind. Pushed by the clear examples of her hostility, she finally shouted defiantly, "Well, I guess I'm a little 'resentful,' but I'm certainly not mad!" We can admit to being "resentful," "hurt," "disappointed," "upset," "peeved," "let down," "teed off," or "put out," but never to being "angry" or "mad."

A rose by any other name would still have thorns! Anger by any other name is just as uncomfortable. Changing its name doesn't work. Like the rose it is still thorny. So next we try denial. We're not angry or hurt. "I don't get angry," we sputter through clenched teeth. But the feeling gets expressed. A group of ministers at a conference recently related half a dozen ways they express their "non-anger": they drive fast, they get ulcers, they work it off, they become depressed, they preach hell-fire and damnation, or they at least bang harder on the lack of commitment, they play aggressively at sports, develop headaches, punish staff members, and they take it out on their wives and families (a wife in the back of the room said, "Amen!"). Often the expressions are completely unconscious—particularly in the marriage relationship. Thoughtlessness, forgetfulness, and ingratitude probably represent anger that isn't openly confronted or acknowledged.

Why is anger so assiduously avoided? The reason is twofold. In the first place, we are not taught how to express it. Rather we are admonished for showing anger and led to believe that we are terribly sinful creatures to feel anger at all. Secondly, anger induces deep within our beings the primitive impulse to react aggressively, ultimately to murder. That's pretty scary. The gutlevel fear of losing control of the primitive drive to destroy demands the lid be screwed on tightly and never lifted off. The fact is that anger is not so destructive as we have come to believe. The walls built between people by unexpressed anger are far more destructive than direct confrontation.

A recently separated couple came in for counseling. The husband discovered that one of his characteristics was to avoid conflict at all cost. The cost finally became the relationship. All the anger and bitterness he felt has been stuffed down inside, creating a thick layer of resentment that is now very difficult to penetrate. But I am encouraged. The other night he began to express some of the resentment. He told his wife things she has been doing that have hurt him for fifteen years. She was completely unaware of his hurt. The confrontation did not drive her away; it drew them closer.

The Bible gives us such practical advice about anger. Jesus saw clearly that a spirit controlled by anger toward one's brother was the root of murder. The anger must not be harbored. He said if we have ill will toward anyone or become conscious that someone may be offended with us, it must be dealt with before we come to the altar. Paul said, "Be angry but sin not," and "Don't let the sun set on your anger." James tells us to be "slow to anger," going on to decry the bitter jealousies, envying, and hate that we hold within ourselves and nurture. Being slow to anger cannot be interpreted as meaning not to show anger at all.

These passages and Jesus' examples teach us that anger is a normal human emotion not to be stockpiled within where it poisons relationships, but to be worked out honestly in a healthy interchange. Thus is relationship restored with man and God.

Fear

What are you afraid of? The board of deacons? Your inner impulses and drives? The insecurity of your future? Being "found out"? We are beset by fears and often can't even identify the object, since it lies below our consciousness. Like guilt, fear (or anxiety) may be normal and even healthy, or it may be neurotic and irrational.

Normal fear produces a creative tension culminating in effective action. You have a speaking engagement or an exam to write, and a certain level of anxiety develops. That's good. You get in gear, study, and write your speech, or prepare for the exam.

Think back for a moment to some event in your life that really scared you. I vividly remember going to a double feature horror movie. The last feature was "The Thing." In the movie a prehistoric monster was accidentally thawed out of a block of ice which had preserved him for hundreds of years.

He went on a destructive rampage and since he was radio-active, the heroes tracked him with Geiger counters. As he came nearer, the speed of the counter's clicks became more rapid in a suspenseful crescendo, climaxed by the beast's bursting into the room.

Well, I don't remember how we finally destroyed the "thing," but I do remember walking briskly all the way home that warm summer night. After going to bed I felt a little safer till I heard a steady crunch, crunch, crunch in the gravel of the neighbors' driveway—just outside my window. I held my breath as I worked up nerve to look out. The streetlight cast an eerie, ever-enlarging, definitely "thing"-shaped shadow on the neighbors' garage door. Then Pat, their son, came into view.

Boy, what a relief! I laughed a nervous laugh and turned over to go to sleep. A cool summer breeze began to blow softly through the open windows and my terror was down to a manageable level. As I was just about to drift away, the Venetian blinds began to click as the wind increased. That clicking was just like those Geiger counters! It began to get faster and I began to count like the scientists in the movie. "Point one, Point two . . . Point nine, Point ten, it's at its peak!" My fantasy was violently punctuated by a loud crash! The summer breeze had become so brisk it had blown the door shut.

In all my life, I'm sure I will never again know fear quite like that. My heart stopped and found its way up into my throat. I couldn't breathe. My muscles all went tense, then rubbery, and I broke out in an instant cold sweat. That is fear. Those are the body's responses as adrenalin is poured out. The reaction is the same whether you are being attacked by "the thing," or by some unconscious dread.

When the fear is of some unknown object, one is overcome by anxiety. Life becomes crippled by an all-pervasive fear that drains one's energy and disrupts his thoughts. Such fear may become attached to a specific situation for the phobic individual, like the fear of heights, or in others it could be free floating and have no defined object. The unconscious process is similar; unacceptable thoughts or impulses become repressed and the feelings attached to them are transferred to other objects. For example, one minister was overcome by anxiety whenever he had deacons' meetings. It was discovered that the chairman of the group reminded him of his overbearing father, and this triggered repressed hostility that threatened to break out of control. Another pastor found himself very anxious in any situation of physical closeness with other men or boys. A fear of homosexual thoughts was discovered. When the real object is identified and faced directly, the fear frequently loses its potency and falls away harmlessly.

Depression

I have never experienced more than a mild degree of depression. I've been "blue" and down in the dumps when things weren't going right. Also I've been sad at the loss of a friend. As have all of us, I've tasted the bitterness of disappointment at being denied some personal goal. But those who have been severely depressed tell me of the utter blackness within. They describe the hopelessness, the inability to plan and act, the point of withdrawal into complete isolation. The depths of that despair are incomprehensible to one who has never traveled its valley. But there are many who know its path.

There are many different and distinct kinds of depression. Some types are determined by an inherited, neurochemical disorder. They have a familial pattern, arising with little or no particular stress. They are cyclical in recurrence and respond to medication. Similarly, involutional depression seems organic in origin, and is most effectively treated by medical or physical means.

Depression may arise from real life situations, such as loss of a loved through death or divorce, the loss of position or influence, and the loss of ability to realize one's life goals.

There are other times when depression derives from unconscious conflicts. The most common such occurrence is the misdirection of anger. Rather than express hostility openly toward its legitimate object, one turns the anger toward self. This is "neurotic" depression.

Neurotic depression may also be generated by unconscious

grief over real or imagined loss. For instance, the mourning for a loved one will sometimes last for many years should the work of grieving be interrupted. Essentially the same process may persist with grief caused by loss of love or approbation. P.K.'s are particularly vulnerable to the latter syndrome, since they repeatedly lose their father's attention but are taught they must not have hard feelings about the loss. To grin and bear it is not always the healthiest mode of coping, but simply delays working through the feelings.

There are several detrimental effects of putting off confrontation. In the first place, the negative feelings, whether anger, guilt, or fear, continue to form an ever-expanding gap between you and your friends or associates. The chasm is harder and harder to bridge, and the relationship may never be rebuilt. All of us know people who were once the best of friends, but who allowed some misunderstanding to come permanently between them long after the original dispute is forgotten!

Second, the unexpressed feelings may easily become displaced. For instance, anger toward a parent may be redirected toward self, resulting in depression, or reflected toward the chairman of the board, who looks like daddy, resulting in a church split.

Finally, a significant degree of emotional energy must be used to keep unwelcomed feelings within. This takes work and uses resources that could be better spent in other more productive ways. I have heard one definition of mental health as keeping the emotional ledgers balanced. Thus one does not let his emotional liabilities stack up, but clears the bills quickly rather than worry about the mounting debts.

Love and Praise

It would be unfair and incomplete to mention only negative feelings. Some of you have just as much trouble in accepting your own positive emotions as in receiving those of others. Are you comfortable with praise, or does your sagging self-esteem quickly neutralize the affirmation offered you?

Love and acceptance must be learned. Tom Harris has

preached this doctrine effectively in *I'm O.K., You're O.K.*
All one must do to get confirmation for his thesis is listen to
parent–child interaction around the supermarket (where folks
don't know you as minister). Do you hear much praise and
acceptance communicated? Not likely. I hear overwhelming
criticism. That may be what you grew up with. I don't agree
that criticism is a universal truth, but the percentage of folks
feeling "not okay" makes me weep. When the image inside
is of an unloved brat, praise is hard to receive. To accept love
one must feel lovable, and to give love we must first feel loved.

Frankly I've been surprised how often ministers are equally
ill-at-ease *giving* praise. I suppose I shouldn't be astonished,
since emotional giving must issue from some reservoir of love.
We have a sort of emotional bank account. During childhood,
deposits of love are made, interest accrues, and we have re-
serves on which to draw for spending on others. Some folks
have a nice balance and learn the invaluable lesson of investment. They invest love lavishly and realize continuous growth
on their capital investment.

Others are poor and always on the verge of bankruptcy.
Since they received meager deposits as children, they remain
distrustful when people try to make contributions later in
their life. They are cautious and defensive, expecting to see
strings attached to every gift. Miserly in their attitude toward
what they have, they hoard it tenaciously. The lesson of in-
vestments was lost to them. Christ put it in terms of sowing
sparingly and reaping sparingly. Such an outlook and stance
does not have to control your life, however. You can come to
know and accept love.

To an individual who has neither been loved nor had his
love accepted in childhood, love may be more threatening
than any other feeling. To express love carries the risk of
having it fall unappreciated, a devastating experience. To have
love offered creates a confusing mixture of emotions: fear
that the offer will be withdrawn, doubt that the love is
genuine, guilt that it is not deserved, and even anger that it
is so late in coming.

21

Expressing Your Emotions

The first step is taken. Are you in contact with your feelings? If so, may I suggest you make a list of them? Now you may be wondering what on earth do I do with them? Find someone to share them with—your wife, an associate, or a friend. It will probably be terrifying to you to reveal for the first time that you have hurts, or doubts, or anger, or fears, or depression, or even love. It will seem unreal to hear your own voice saying the words, "I just wanted to share some feelings I've become aware of. Lately I've been really anxious, and I don't understand why."

Take it slowly. It's risky business at first. Trust must be built. Start with the least threatening feelings and go from there. You will be overjoyed at how good it feels to be a human being, to climb down from the pedestal and unmask a little.

Those of you who are married should include your spouse fairly early in the process. If your marriage relationship is cool and distant, or non-existent, that is not the place for you to start this unmasking. If a relationship is ever to be built, however, honest intimate sharing must occur—at some point when you have become more adept at giving and receiving feelings. For the happy person who already enjoys real marital intimacy, this open exposure can deepen and enrich the relationship.

Some of you may look at the prospect of verbalizing your feelings, even to your best friend, as too threatening. The wounds may seem too painful to uncover. A professional counselor will provide your best opportunity for beginning the unveiling. Many facilities are now available to you which offer anonymity, confidentiality, and expertise.

22

Unweighting

We live in ski country. I didn't know where the Lord might finally place us, but I tell folks when you leave your destiny in His hands, you have to be prepared for whatever comes. The risk is great—you might end up a few miles from Aspen, Colorado. If that happens, a heavy obligation falls on your shoulders. How can you avoid learning to ski? Those of you who have experienced downhill skiing will recall the sheer terror of facing a sudden mogul field that seems to drop endlessly and precipitously out from under your skis. As you learn to ski you discover that to change direction and maintain control you must master the technique of "unweighting." Your weight must be lifted from the skis to enable you to execute the turn. It is essential. It requires practice and timing.

What has all this ski talk to do with a minister and his problems? Well, I see many pastors running dangerously out of control down the steep slopes of their existence. They are terrified and holding on for dear life, knowing they are headed for a wipe out, but unable to get their skis to change directions. They haven't learned "unweighting." The weight that prevents the maneuver is the burden of unrealistic expectations they have accepted. We have discussed these in some detail. Now let's look at how to unload.

When I first put on skis I had absolutely no idea what the instructors were talking about when they began insisting on a certain weight distribution, forward, back, downhill ski, uphill ski, etc. Before I could regulate anything I had to realize for myself what effect the weight had, and I even had to overcome some natural tendencies and habit patterns. So it is with you. First you must realize what weights you carry and where the pressure is applied. Are you constantly off balance because you try to bend to fit everyone's demands? Are your own inner standards so rigid you have no freedom of movement? Diagnose your problems. You may even want to make a list of the expectations you try to meet. For instance, your list might look something like this:

1. I must always be right.
2. I can't say no to any request.
3. I have to visit every church family at least monthly.
4. I should not take a day off completely.
5. I must be a good administrator (teacher, preacher, pastor, fund-raiser, etc.).
6. I must be sinless.

Now ask where those standards are coming from, without or within? Are they realistic or not? Why must you fit the mold? You will find that some standards you've accepted cannot be compromised. That's okay. Others are negotiable, and some are simply stupid! What would you have to do to eliminate the ridiculous ones immediately? Do it! What about those that seem open to compromise or scrutiny? Will you need to discuss them with someone? Try your wife. She knows you better than you can imagine. With the right approach she might even be honest with you. Your staff will be delighted to enlighten you as to your unrealistic expectations and demands. They are aware of the burden you carry, and, chances are, they have been trying to help you "unweight" for years.

23

Understanding Your Worth

Al Westendorf is a psychiatrist in Michigan. At a recent conference he commented that those who have never known love from man are incapable of understanding God's love and grace. He is right. Christians understand that every man is intrinsically and infinitely valuable by virtue of his creation in the image of God, and that God esteems men highly as evidenced by his sacrificial death on the cross.

I see men of God who preach love and forgiveness and have an intellectual understanding of grace, but are unable to apply it to their own lives. Because of early life rejection they feel worthless and condemned. They never grasp the truth and joy of being: the beauty of living as a unique creature made in the image of God, redeemed by his love, and freed from the slavery of self-centeredness. On they trudge in an endless cycle of seeking, yet rejecting, affirmation. The truth is, they are not actually looking for affirmation as a unique and valuable individual, but confirmation of the failure image they treasure so dearly. To deny *that* self (the failure) might accuse daddy of being wrong all along, and that's too big a risk to the child within. Furthermore, to creep out from under the rock might entail really exposing oneself and being accepted. Why should that be bad? Because they don't believe they can produce! They're right. They can't. Not up to the inhuman goals they have adopted. But hold on to your chair; I have a startling announcement. *You* will be accepted as *you*, warts and all.

I know what some of you are saying: "Well, that sounds good, but he doesn't know me. I have failed at more things than he can imagine!" Maybe you're right. If you feel that way, you're not ready to accept freedom. You are still too caught up in self. That's right; you're self-centered, dedicated to proving that you are the greatest failure of all time. When you are tired of that game, you'll be willing to take the risk of discovering the real you, and finding life when self is finally denied.

24

Priorities

After your rebirth as an individual of worth who struggles with feelings like the rest of the human race, an important task confronts you. To avoid losing all you've gained, you must reevaluate your priorities. Many of the old activities that have been so critical will lose their meaning in the light of your new expectations. You will not only discover that you are dispensable, but you will find that fact no longer threatens you.

Where have your priorities been? This is a good time for another list. If you're the typical minister, you've been a "workaholic" married to the church. I'll let you in on a secret—she's already married! You may not only be trying to supplant the Bridegroom, but if you're a married man, you have been unfaithful to your wife.

I can find no Scripture text that excludes you from the commands regarding the responsibilities of husband and father just because you are ordained. Besides the clear obligation toward those responsibilities, you have an obligation to yourself. We have the example of Christ who took time to be alone, to gain strength, spiritual and physical, with which to minister. If Jesus, the very Son of God, needed that renewing, it's okay for you and me. He never even apologized after one of those absences from the disciples and the crowds. Can't you just hear it now: Jesus, returning from the mountains and gathering together the multitude unto himself, said, "Please forgive me for tarrying so long. I am sorely grieved that I had to be away. I'd not have departed at all, knowing how thou needest me, but there was this important conference I had to attend with my supervisor. But be not afraid, I won't be away again until next year." He didn't even seem guiltridden when

Mary and Martha reminded him that in his absence their brother, Lazarus, had died. (Sorrowful, yes; guilty, no.)

When you can reestablish your priorities, you will discover a remarkable new effectiveness in your life. May I urge you to do so, and to share these decisions with your congregation? If they cannot accept you with the changes you are led to make, perhaps they need tender, caring education. I am convinced that when they see you as a more human brother with the same needs and problems they experience, they will accept you more completely. Not only you, but the spiritual truths you are prepared to offer.

An exciting new ministry awaits you as you find freedom from the heavy load under which you've been struggling, and truly discover his easy yoke.

Part VI

The Minister's Wife

Wives, be subject to your husbands as to the Lord. . . . Husbands, love your wives, as Christ also loved the church and gave himself up for it . . . (Eph. 5:22, 25 NEB).

Have you ever wondered about Peter's wife? We don't even know if she was still living—we hear only about her mother. If she weren't living, I suspect I know what killed her. She was a preacher's wife! I have imagined the conversations around the manse in Capernaum:

"Lydia, dear, where is Simon? I haven't seen him for days."

"Your guess is as good as mine, mother. I wish he'd go back to fishing. I knew where he was then—either out in that stinking boat, or down at the Jolly Sailor with those Zebedee boys."

"Is he still following Jesus around?"

"Yes, he is obsessed with that man. He has left everything to chase after him. I don't think he gives me a thought any more, and we can barely make ends meet. I think I'll go to work. That'll help support us and keep me from losing my mind."

"But, dear, Jesus may be the Messiah. Simon thinks so. You shouldn't feel that way. What an honor that he called Simon to follow him."

"Well, he didn't call me!"

It has been going on ever since. A radiant young maiden falls in love with a handsome fisherman or seminarian, manages to get caught by him, and promises to love, honor, and cherish. Then he enters the pastorate and life takes a sudden and drastic turn. For three long years in seminary she has worked and struggled to help him get educated, eagerly anticipating graduation and their first church. What she expects of that is anyone's guess—but it seldom turns out to be what she had dreamed about. If she rarely saw him during seminary, now she sees him even less. If he was preoccupied and had little time for her then, now he has less. If the budget was tight then, it's tighter now. If the pressure was high then, it's now practically unbearable. To make matters worse, she finds they have grown apart spiritually and intellectually, now that he is a "theologian." She finds herself married to a stranger, perhaps burdened by a growing family, and thrust into a role created by a select jury of busybodies dedicated to the task of rearranging her life.

We can't fully approach the problem of the ministry without looking at the difficulties the wife must face and how they affect her relationship with her husband.

25

The Pressures

I'm painting a dismally depressing picture, and I realize it is not always so bad. If your marriage is joyous and your relationship marked by a warm sharing of life's adventures, just disregard what is to follow. But hold it. Not too fast. Before you declare yourself exempt from problems, maybe you should ask your wife. I've been amazed at how little awareness many ministers have of the wife's feelings. If at this point you don't have the courage to ask her, just keep reading.

The minister's wife shares all the pressures and pitfalls that beset her husband, and she is a victim on two levels. As an individual, she feels the loneliness and isolation, the fear and insecurity, the unexpressed hostility, the effects of poverty, etc. Then all of those sensitive wounds are compounded as she shares her husband's hurts.

The Minister's Masculine Approach

Most men either are not sensitive to their wife's distress, or they deny it because they feel impotent to offer a solution. Men are uncomfortable with any problem they cannot "fix" on the spot, but frequently these are the kinds of issues your wife brings up to you. Most of you will go to great lengths to avoid such conflicts, leaving your wives to somehow cope on their own. This is a typical masculine approach. Remember, you're the one we have been describing as a loner who holds everything inside through denial or rationalization. Feelings are foreign currency you never learned to spend. So when your wife comes crying, you get mad because you feel the pressure to make everything okay, and you can't do it. You just don't have the sensitivity to feelings, or an ability to verbalize them freely.

The female you married is quite the opposite. Women *are* different—there is no such thing as unisex. She can hold things in and deny them just so long; then she must talk it out, if not to you, to someone else. Last spring we led a retreat for pastors' wives. Seventy or eighty women unloaded to each other and to us. There weren't many barriers to prevent that group from talking it out. The main one was their reluctance to expose the husband's faults and failings. The most frequent complaint was loss of individual identity and privacy.

Sharon's Story

Sharon was typical. A young, vivacious, capable woman, she reflected the feelings of the younger generation.

"I would like for people to relate to me as 'Sharon,' and not just the preacher's wife. I have likes and dislikes, joy and pain, doubts and fears like everyone else, but it seems that nobody cares about 'me'! Most of them don't even know I have a name."

Your wife is probably less caught up in the role-playing and image-fitting than you are, so she is not as bound by the expectations. And yet, it isn't so much the unreasonable things she is called on to do—secretary, pianist, nursery worker, and maid—as the way she is asked to comply that bugs her. "Sharon" was not asked to do any of the tasks because of *her* ability, but because she was the "preacher's wife."

Loss of privacy is closely related to this problem. Not only is the preacher's wife property of the church, but so are his house and family. I never cease to be surprised at the liberties church members take with your privacy. A few years ago one wife was telling us of life next door to the church in a parsonage which was the well-worn shortcut from the parking lot to the sanctuary. Dinner parties and family Christmases were interrupted by troops of intruders who didn't knock and acted resentful that the pathway was cluttered.

Her husband tried locks and even jamming the door. To

this action one helpful old gentleman replied, "Preacher, that back door has been stickin', but I just fixed it for you! Shouldn't cause you any more grief!"

To top that, a wife who had lived above a storefront mission was awakened one morning by a couple of ladies looking for the pastor—in their bedroom. The word got around that the preacher and his wife sure did sleep late!

In addition to those common pressures and her husband's pains, the preacher's wife must face the same issue confronting the wife of the executive or doctor: the loss of her mate. She rarely has a moment with you alone. You fight the battle for a living and for a sense of accomplishment in your vocation. Your wife seeks her fulfilment primarily in the context of the home. Thus the stage is set for the most common conflict—how each of you can achieve self-satisfaction, support one another, and even become one. The wife's desire to succeed as a helpmate dictates that she maintain the feeling of being a part of your life and interest. Her efforts to break into your daily work routine to attain this goal may appear to be an effort to run your life, and may be extremely threatening to you. This fear forces you to retreat further into that other world. A destructive cycle is established, often ending with complete alienation and hatred. Jim Mallory has an excellent discussion of this marital pattern in *The Kink and I.**

To make matters worse, your spouse must overcome another obstacle. You are neglecting her—not for another woman, not to make money, not for drinking buddies, but for *the church*. This situation creates tremendous tension. She knew when you were married that you were dedicated to the ministry, but few wives anticipate the degree of neglect they come to feel. They become bitter, beginning to resent you and the church, and then they may feel guilty because of the anger they feel.

One wife put it this way, "I wish it *were* another woman, I could go pull her hair out!" She can't fight it out on equal ground with the church.

---

* James Mallory, Jr., *The Kink and I*, Victor Press, Wheaton (1975).

The Two Types of Ministers' Wives

There seem to be two basic types of ministers' wives. One feels called to be a pastor's wife and shares enthusiastically in his dedication and involvement. The other fell in love with a particular fellow and wants to give her life to being his wife, and the mother of his children. There's nothing wrong with either position.

There also seem to be two basic types of minister-husbands. The one wants his wife to share his work and stand at his side throughout his ministry, helping in various phases. The other resents such involvement and really prefers his wife to be a helpmate at home, caring for his personal needs and for their family. There is nothing wrong with either of these attitudes.

When wife type A marries husband type B, however, something's got to give. These mismatches occur with regrettable regularity and are aggravated by the capricious whims of congregation C who may want an associate today, a pastor's wife tomorrow, both next week, and neither next month!

Phil and Betty had real problems in this category. Betty was highly motivated to be a leader in "their" ministry. She was convinced that she functioned better than Phil in several areas. That was part of the problem. She did. He saw her as more a threat to his control and authority than as a helpmate. He actually did need her help, but he was afraid to accept it. What developed was a yo-yo-ing role for her, alternately being drawn up into the action, then let down with a jolt when her presence became too dangerous. She resented not only being dropped from the church duties periodically, but also her alternate role of mother, which was uncomfortable for her.

Susan's Story

Susan, by contrast, married her man—not the ministry—and wanted dearly just to be a homemaker. She resisted his every effort and those of the church to enlist her as associate. Neither Susan nor her husband had been willing to give up or compromise significantly on his individual role preference for her. He persisted in trying to force her into the work, and she stubbornly refused to be recruited. Consequently, a smoldering fire of discontent and tension pervaded their home. One would expect these kinds of conflicts to be openly discussed and differences negotiated. All too often they are never exposed, much less talked out. It was not so difficult for Susan and Mark to work out some compromises, once they realized the problem.

Barbara's Hang-up

Another little-discussed area of potential pressure in most homes is sex. The minister's wife is not exempt from the common disappointments and battles of the bedroom. Actually, because of the Victorian approach to sexuality that still pervades many Christian homes, the problems may be intensified. The attempt to assure premarital chastity frequently contributes to lifelong frigidity. In our regrettable culture of the double standard, it is often the woman whose enjoyment and fulfilment is most impaired. She learned the lesson well—sex is sin. But they forgot to teach her all the lesson—sex is also fun and ordained by God.

I have had several wives in therapy who expressed what Barbara embarrassingly confessed. "Dr. McBurney," she stammered, growing more crimson as she began to whisper, "I've got this real hang-up about sex. I feel dirty when we have sex. Joe wants to do things that seem wrong to me, and when we're through he wants to be naked the rest of the night. I feel like I want to get something on immediately to cover my shame."

Barbara went on to share her early life experiences regarding sex, and it became apparent why she had "hang-ups." Not only did her mother and her church teach her that sex was dirty and at best a necessary evil, but she had been sexually molested at the age of ten, which was a terrifying experience.

No one had bothered to discuss the healthy Christian view of sex and help her overcome the stigma of the sin-label that was imbedded within her consciousness.

Of course, not all wives have such a damaged outlook on

sex. The hang-ups they report may be different: "He doesn't care about my needs so long as he is satisfied"; "We don't seem to be turned on at the same time. He wants sex when I'm exhausted, and I'm ready when he has to go to some meeting"; "I don't feel attractive and sexy anymore because he's never interested." "What's all right (i.e. morally approved) to do in love-making? Sometimes I enjoy something that seems sinful"; or "My husband had an affair with his secretary, and I can never forgive him and let him touch me again."

The main sexual hang-up is not a matter of technique or frequency, but is the attitude about communicating our sexual desires and fears. The vast majority of sexual problems in marriage can be solved by talking them out. When the communication breaks down (or is never established), sexual fulfilment will be sacrificed, and sexual union is a significant part of "becoming one flesh."

26

Blowing Off the Steam

Have you ever planned an important project or event and found the whole scheme submarined by your mate? She was so dreadfully sorry, but "she forgot all about it." Have you ever had an important engagement and found that you had no clean shirt—again? Have you been dissatisfied with your wife's housekeeping efforts, only to meet with apologies and promises that are never kept? Have you found your sexual relationship deteriorating, but have not been able to discover the reason? All of these behaviors may represent the same communication. Her "forgetfulness" and uncooperativeness could be her only way of expressing her hostility and resentment—resentment that is generated by your "forgetfulness" and nonsupport of her.

Jim and Joyce were having problems in their marriage for the "first time" in its ten-year history. Joyce was painfully and vocally aware of all his shortcomings, but she did not believe she was contributing to the problem because he rarely complained. I asked her what was the one thing he would most like her to change. She answered immediately, "To be a better housekeeper, but that's not really the big issue." Later, when I interviewed Jim and asked him what bugged him about Joyce, the first thing he said was, "She is a sloppy housekeeper! I've hinted and even asked that she change, but she won't. It drives me crazy." They had no open conflict for ten years, only a constant building of pressure. She expressed her resentment only through her refusal to improve her housekeeping, a potent weapon.

Bill and Martha married and had four children. He was met at home with constant criticism. Either there was a list of projects he had ignored, or incessant castigation for his always being away. He was conscious of his desire to schedule church work as often as possible to avoid the hassles and put-downs at home. His wife's attempts to gain a foothold only served to drive him further into his main defense, avoidance. He had become locked into a routine of spending more and more time away from home until they finally separated.

Not all women will resort to such open tactics as nagging or fighting back. A more subtle system is that of warfare through the children. The wife's bitterness and resentment is unconsciously transplanted into the children. They become mom's spokesmen and warriors, doing battle by their misbehavior, school problems, or rejection of their father.

The Pattern Emerges

Mary, who was totally unaware of this pattern, confided, "Sometimes I think he deserves all the grief they can give him." I am confident they received her message and dutifully obeyed, although she thought she had never verbalized it directly to them. One daughter caused constant turmoil at home with her emotional outbursts and another with school problems and running away. Mary also said she had quit trying to express her anger directly toward her husband years ago because she just couldn't stand the conflict.

These patterns are not consciously and maliciously conceived, but they are nonetheless destructive. Many of you can be justifiably proud that this kind of turmoil doesn't mar your marriage, but don't relax yet. I've left what is probably the most common problem until last—psychosomatic illness.

The body is affected by our emotions. Anyone who watches TV knows about Excedrin headaches #25, #32, and #11:00 A.M. Sunday. Our tensions either find release outwardly or take their toll on body functions. At the Mayo Clinic our psychiatry section was born and nourished by this physiological fact. We rarely had patients who came to see *us*. They came to the internists or surgeons because of headaches, stomach trouble, bowel disorders, back pain, skin rashes, or heart attacks. Understandably, many had been to doctors for years and received treatment for the various possible causes of their symptoms. Finally, at the Mayo Clinic they would learn the truth: the illness was emotional.

Dutiful Carolyn

Carolyn is a model minister's wife. She considers herself to be the prime candidate for the Submissive Wife of the Year award. She tolerates an unbelievable degree of neglect and lack of consideration from her husband, who is sensitive to everyone's needs but hers. She does so without complaint; yea, she declares even without resentment. She never nags. She creates an admirable father image of him with the children. She is a dutiful wife in every respect except when her stomach is "acting up again." She has consulted several specialists. The physical findings have been highly questionable, but her denial of any emotional problems has made a psychiatric approach impossible. The only time her husband is attentive and available is when she is bedfast. Then he waits on her, cares for the children, and shows interest in *her*. That's a lot of secondary gain to give up, especially when psychotherapy would force her to face the repressed anger that threatens to emerge.

One other means of blowing off the steam can't be overlooked. It can be more destructive than any of the rest. It is for the wife to attack her husband in public. The main reason for cutting down your mate before an audience is to gain either safety or sympathy. Couples who snipe at each other are frequently unable to fight it out in private. One or the other is so afraid of conflict that he clams up or storms out, leaving both with simmering rage. The pressure mounts until it can be safely blown off. Only in the presence of some buffer do they find that safety. Among friends they feel that the anger can be vented but won't get out of hand. They may even veil the hostility with humor to entertain the guests. It is rarely entertaining, even if the guests laugh.

The desire for sympathy as a motive for cutting hubby down to size derives from the bitterness engendered by the praise and acceptance lavished on him by his flock. The wife is thinking, *If these people really knew what a self-centered louse he is, they would treat me with the respect and admiration I deserve.*

Facing Hostility Honestly

Eleanor would steam, just thinking about the way the church members worshiped her husband. She knew how imperfect he was. He was selfish and inconsiderate, gave her little help with the children, would pout or walk out if anyone got in his way, and made life miserable for everyone in the family. They would go to a party and she would boil as his flock expressed their love for him. A part of her wanted to share the warmth, but the rest of her burned with desire to expose him as a fraud. That part usually won out, and she would begin her exposé. He would desert her and spend the evening avoiding her stinging "wit." His avoidance intensified her resentment and sharpened her tongue.

Fortunately, hostility can be faced honestly without guilt. It may even be eliminated altogether. The secret is in re-·evaluating the expectations to which you subscribe, and becoming aware of what is happening in your relationship. You don't "have to be" always available to the church, but you must be a husband. You are commanded to leave parents and *become one* with your wife, to love her even as Christ loved the church.

One minister at a marriage enrichment retreat had reasoned that since he was commanded to deny himself, and his wife was one with him, then he was obligated to deny her needs along with his own. To plug that reasoning into Paul's analogy of Christ and the church would be to say that Jesus was to deny the church—the bride for which he died. The bride was high on Jesus' priority list. If that priority pertained to our Lord and the church, does it not also apply to you and your wife—even if you are a minister? By the way, it was Jesus who married the church—not you.

It was also Christ who said, "The truth shall make you free." This holds true for the marriage relationship. Don't be afraid to find out what's going on. The true feelings you have

can be faced and worked through with a new freedom for becoming one. Most couples I counsel have been avoiding the
truth for years. They are so afraid to look honestly at themselves that they often delay until there is little left of the
marriage. Several factors contribute to this fear. I believe the
most important is the reluctance to admit, "I may not be
doing it right." After all, you are the man of God!

Part VII

The Forgotten Begotten

The time came when God put Abraham to the test. "Abraham," he called, and Abraham replied, "Here I am." God said, "Take your son Isaac, your only son, whom you love, and go to the land of Moriah. There you shall offer him as a sacrifice on one of the hills which I will show you" (Gen. 22:1, 2 NEB).

As far as I can tell, that's the last time God asked a father to sacrifice his son, with one exception. The exception, of course, was his completed act on Calvary, and that was done only with the Son's consent. Yet I repeatedly see sons and daughters sacrificed on the altar of dad's service to God.

Mike is now in his 20s and has left home. When we first met, he was a high school student expressing his rebellion by poor school performance, drug abuse, and complete rejection of the church. A large part of the anger that motivated his misbehavior came from his experiences as a P.K. (Preacher's Kid). He complained that he never had a father. Family plans for vacation, or father-son fishing trips were all too often postponed indefinitely because of the demands of the church. He said he just couldn't compete with the church members for his dad's attention.

Mike and his parents learned to communicate and found out some fascinating things about each other. Happily, their relationship improved and Mike's rebellious behavior lost its value to him. His resentment toward the church has persisted longer than that toward his parents, but even that has mellowed.

Let's look at the normal stages of childhood development

and at some commonly encountered circumstances confronting the pastor's child. At each stage I will review some specific positive and negative aspects of childrearing in the pastor's home, then deal with more general topics of concern for all parents.

27

Infancy

In this vital stage of development a child first comes to feel either accepted and loved, or resented and rejected—feelings that may strongly influence all his future relationships. Erik Erickson describes the major task of this period as developing trust. The infant asks, "Can I depend on these big people around me to take care of my needs?"

The positive values brought to bear in your home are significant. In general, ministers and their wives are more highly educated and are aware of the importance of infant care. The baby is likely the product of planned pregnancy, good prenatal care, obstetrical attention during labor and delivery, and early pediatric consultation. Proper nutrition is assured, as well as a clean, wholesome house. The baby probably receives warmth and affection not only from you but also from the church members.

The negative facets of the pastorate are those common to most young families. The financial situation may require that the mother work, thus preventing her from spending all her time with the baby. The demands of seminary or early pastorates may also infringe on the availability of both of you. The emotional strain on you and on your relationship during these years may seriously impair your ability to cope with the dependency needs of the baby.

Unreasonable Expectations

The most regrettable factor, which will have its effect throughout childhood, is your unreasonable expectations of yourselves. Since you think you must be able to do everything just right, with never a bad thought, you typically feel you can't ask advice about childrearing, or admit frustration and resentments. You frequently cannot even share with each other the awful stress that you feel. If you were free to discuss the problems, you would find that even "the experts," such as the family physician, child psychiatrist, or pediatrician, don't always have the "right answer."

Not having the right answer can cause deep despair. Remember those two o'clock feedings and the crying of a colicky baby? I do, and not always with pleasure! It wasn't easy always to be happy about that little bundle of joy sent by God. It's harder yet to cope with those emotions if you don't permit yourself to admit the resentment, anger, and hostile impulses as normal and acceptable. Having those feelings doesn't mean you don't love and cherish that helpless, demanding creature with the wet, dirty diapers and the perpetual appetite.

As parents of that new life, you may struggle with many fears and questions. With the first baby, one of your greatest concerns will be, "What is normal?" The baby seems hungry every hour, or he sleeps too long. His bowels seem too loose, his urine, too strong. He seems to spit up too much, or burp too loudly. Hundreds of behaviors raise the question.

The common reaction is that you should know what is normal, so you are not free to admit that you wonder. Believe me, every new parent grapples with those doubts. When our first baby was born I was a sophomore in medical school. I had begun to study pediatrics and had access to the basic textbooks. The trouble was they dealt with the weighty issues —proper motor development, nutritional requirements, infant mortality, pediatric pathology, and congenital malformations. They didn't say how runny the bowel movement ought to be, or how loud a burp, and I wasn't about to ask!

That created a problem. Melissa expected me, her resident doctor, to have all the answers. She soon learned I was as ignorant as all other fathers of newborn babies. But we were curious enough to compare notes with those other new parents. Those conversations, along with her lists of questions for the pediatrician, proved to be an acceptable way to learn.

The Advantages of the Extended Family

In the former days of the extended family, some grand-mother, sister, or aunt would have taught us. Now, however, few couples have their families available other than the two-week visit from one of the grandmothers immediately after the birth. If you don't have your extended family, however, you can adopt one. There are plenty of grandmothers in most churches who will gladly answer these "stupid" questions and relieve the doubts if you are honest enough to ask.

Another common problem is the fear of failure. You fathers especially may be scared to death of that fragile creature, so rather than risk holding him improperly or appearing nervous and clumsy, you may avoid having anything to do with the infant at all. "Wait till he can catch a ball, then I'll play with him," is your rationalization.

That is really sad. In the first place, your wife needs the emotional support of seeing you involved with this new being the two of you created. Your avoidance may be interpreted as rejection of what she has given you, and that is an important concern of hers. She has produced a baby: conceived it in love, carried it in her own body, endured the pain of de-livery, struggled with the fears of whether it would be normal and whether she might die giving it life, and has found the gratifying completion of her womanhood. She offers you this priceless gift and waits for your response.

Besides that highly significant emotional need, she could use some help. It isn't easy to cope singlehandedly with the 24-hour-a-day demands of an infant. There are many things you can do as father.

My first advice is to encourage your wife to breast-feed the baby. Then you *can't* get up at 2 A.M., warm the bottle, change the diaper, feed and burp the little critter! *But* as a loving husband you *can* bring the baby to the "bottle," and burp him before putting him back to bed—while your wife sleeps on and loves you more and more.

Getting Involved

You can also change a diaper now and then, and maybe even put a load into the washer. It won't hurt you a bit. And one of the joys you must not miss is feeding your baby strained spinach. Bruce learned how to blow bubbles with it. That is something to experience—spinach bubbles splattering in your face. Andrea was more delicate. As befits a dainty little girl, she did graceful finger painting on the high chair, tray, her cheeks, and my arm. Brent was his own man. He found unique and surprising ways to get the spinach into his hair—with the spoon, his hand, or the whole bowl—in a flash there it would be again—the boy with green hair.

When you have spooned out the spinach a time or two, you're "involved."

Another important reason for your involvement, even at that early age, is that your baby has begun to record in his subconscious all the messages about "love" and "trust" and "caring" which remain with him *forever*. Think about the significance of that trust, and you won't say, "Wait till he can catch a ball."

28

The Toddler

The terrible two's are fascinating—looking back. But they can be a nightmare to endure. In this period the child begins to truly differentiate "self" from "other." He has new found motor skills and mobility. Coupled with the curiosity that has always been there, the combination creates constant chaos and calamity. The toddler not only discovers his freedom of movement, but the freedom of his will.

For one to exercise his own will he must first say "no," for to say "yes" accedes to the desires of the "other." The emerging individuality of a two-year-old cannot tolerate such submission. He says "no" automatically and digs in his heels to get his own way.

Parsonage Life Has Its Advantages . . .

For a toddler life in the parsonage has some particular benefits. His environment will most likely be clean and safe, and his parents sensitive to his physical needs. Equally important is the intellectual stimulation he receives. His parents are interested in verbal skills and will probably talk to him and begin to introduce him to books. It has been shown that reading to toddlers, even from material beyond their comprehension, increases their verbal abilities. The importance of toys to his motor development is realized, and he will be allowed freedom to explore his environment.

And Disadvantages

The negatives begin to multiply rapidly, too. At this critical stage, when the expanding personality needs freedom within a framework of consistent, secure limits, an unstable state of changing expectations and restrictions presents itself. The confusing effects of too many parents invade in various forms, for your child is more likely to be cared for by a succession of volunteers. Either in the church nursery, in homes of willing church members, or at various committee meetings, he may become everyone's child. Some of these "baby-sitters" will dote and encourage misbehavior, and some will be rigid and severe in their limits and their punishment. Meanwhile, you and your wife may feel too insecure in your position (as the pastor's family and as new parents) to properly structure your toddler's environment. Everyone's responsibility may become no one's, and serious behavior problems may be in the making.

Too much mobility and too disruptive a schedule are additional dangers. Children are resilient and can survive a remarkable degree of chaos if they have the dependable, secure relationship of loving parents. But at a time when they are just establishing "self," they need stability of environment. A daily routine with rest, play, and the important time with mother and daddy allows them to master each new skill, then progress to new challenges in a comfortable continuum. But alas, many ministers' schedules are so crowded with activities that the needed quiet and rest are never found—for anyone.

The most characteristic features of the toddler are his sudden mobility and his negativism. In looking at general features of childrearing, we must address these.

Mobility with Limits

You must expect your toddler to get to *anything* he wants or *any place* he decides to go. I'll never forget the day after we brought Andrea home from the hospital. Bruce was 2½ and very interested in his new sister, and we encouraged him to love her and be a good big brother. We had just put her into her baby bed—regulation size, with the side rails up. Melissa, my mother-in-law, and I were sitting in the living room probably talking about the first granddaughter when Bruce came in—carrying Andrea in his arms like a rag doll. Don't ask me how he got her out of that bed. I'm just glad I didn't see it happen. She was unhurt, and we learned that a two-year-old can be very resourceful.

If one could restrict the mobility of children, and I doubt that is possible, it would be detrimental to their development. What is necessary is to make the way safe. Provide room for them to climb and explore with the dangers removed. It is important to remember that they do not set restrictions on themselves or always recognize dangers. You must provide the limits. A two-year-old is barely beginning to learn not to play in streets or cross them. His curiosity will lead him anywhere, and he still tastes most things. You must control his environment.

Negativism

Tell a toddler to do anything and he will usually say, "No." He's not trying to frustrate you and make your life miserable. He is simply exercising his will, which he is just discovering. It takes him some time to figure out that "yes" can also reflect his will.

A happy way to avoid the hassle of trying to change his will is to offer choices. Do you want "this" or "that"? Would you rather sleep "here" or "there"? It is easier to distract a toddler than to challenge him. Of course, there are going to be inevitable collisions of will, and at those times it is important to remember that you are the parent and try not to let your emotional response be as violent as his.

This is the time to begin setting limits and making them stick. And it is essential that both parents operate together. If you begin to encourage cute little misdemeanors, or your wife is oversolicitous after daddy has enforced a limit, a dangerous pattern may be quickly established that is not so quickly overcome. Become aware of the dynamics of the situation and consciously build a loving and secure relationship.

29

The Preschool Years

The terrible two's finally give way to more pleasant times During the preschool years your child is developing an im portant balance between initiative and control. On the one hand, he is beginning to plan out a course of action. On the other, he is beginning to set some limits on those actions, that is, his conscience, or superego, is emerging. The "do's" and "don'ts" he has been hearing from others are becoming a part of himself. Now when he contemplates putting mud in little sister's hair, or sand in the gas tank of your car, a voice inside may remind him he shouldn't do that.

Social Interaction

Another important aspect of this period is his broadening social interaction. The preschooler no longer struggles so stubbornly to assert his individuality. He is beginning to be secure as a self, and he can cooperate with others. The children begin to play *together* rather than simply alongside one another.

During these years P.K.'s have the advantage of social involvement with other children. They are usually involved in Sunday school and frequently in preschool programs. Here they learn to share and find out that others have rights just as they do. They begin to discover cooperation, doing things in a group. For the first time, they begin to tune in to the feed-back of the environment. Their boundaries have expanded and how others respond takes on meaning.

At this stage of personality development the child is learning initiative. He contemplates actions and plans how to carry them through. He also learns to exercise internal controls over those fantasized exploits. Conscience—the superego—is taking shape. The child can become overcontrolled by a rigid superego and beset by guilt over the contemplated actions. Many of you have had that experience in life, and you struggle now with this need for control.

P.K.'s also have the advantage of exposure to a social institution with moral concern. They are taught the biblical principles of right and wrong. In our culture of situation ethics and television violence, it is important that we teach them some solid foundations for living as responsible, concerned adults.

The liability side of the ledger for the P.K. reveals two opposing dangers, that of overcontrols and occasionally that of fostering certain behavior that reflects an absence of internal (superego) controls. Let's examine each of these.

The P.K.'s Burden

The expectations that the preacher's child be a paragon of virtue may place an unreasonable burden on him. The lists of do's and don't's of some groups may far exceed the absolutes of God's laws, and the joy of grace becomes lost in legalism. He may easily become excessively scrupulous and inhibited, and he may establish a lifelong pattern of guilt and compulsivity.

In extreme cases these problems may show up in childhood, with a child being very clean and obedient and beginning to have compulsive behavior. For instance, a handwashing or cleaning ritual may appear. This type of behavior develops as an attempt to undo or protect against "unclean" thoughts or impulses. A child who has been given severe restrictions and has been shamed for thoughts or activities which were normal will be particularly vulnerable. The guilt that is thus spawned may follow him all his life.

The 'Runaway' Syndrome

The other side of the coin is a fascinating one. Highly controlled, moralistic parents may unconsciously foster certain misbehavior in their children. Those of you who could never express rebellion toward the system may get vicarious pleasure in seeing your child "give it to 'em." Dr. Adelaide Johnson at the Mayo Clinic identified this process as creating "super-ego lacunae"—holes in the conscience. One of her earliest cases was a child who ran away, and not just around the block. He would be found across town. It was noticed that his father seemed more proud than distressed by his son's adventurous streak. It was learned that the father had always fantasized leaving his job and responsibilities and hitting the road. He unconsciously encouraged his son to act out his own repressed desire.

I have seen a family with a similar problem. They have a rebellious child who is, I believe, responding to her father's unmet needs to rebel. He grew up in a neighborhood filled with parent-figures who assured his staying within the rigid rules of the community. Now as she throws off the social restraints, surrounding her, he glows with admiration. She is pulling off what he was never able to do. Some of you, P.K.'s yourselves, have similar backgrounds. Unconsciously, you may encourage your offspring's mischief.

Let's look now at some general features of this period of development. The preschooler is a sponge for knowledge. He can absorb about as much as you can take the time to teach him, so take that time! Don't allow the television to baby-sit him all day. The studies are conclusive; most T.V. programming is violent—even children's shows—and those programs have the effect of increasing violence and aggressive behavior in the viewer. This has been shown conclusively in psychological studies involving over 10,000 children.[*] If you can adequately control the viewing in your home, that's good. If you can't, as we couldn't consistently do, get rid of your T.V. We did that about four years ago and are elated by the change. Our children now read books, play games, and come up with their own creative images, rather than simply reflecting the latest T.V. commercials.

---

[*] M. B. Rothenberg, *Effect of Television Violence on Children*, Youth Journal of the American Medical Association, Volume 234, No. 10, pages 1043–1046.

Now I'll get off my favorite soapbox and move on to another critical area. The preschooler still needs controls. It will not warp his developing ego for you to be firm in setting limits. He will learn quickly whether or not you mean business when you say "no." The Bible says, "Provoke not your children to wrath." One way to honor that commandment is to be reasonable and consistent. Don't make unrealistic demands and repeated hollow threats. I hear parents nag their children relentlessly.

"If you don't stop that, I'll . . ." The child continues, but ". . ." never happens. Instead he gets, "Didn't you hear me? I said, 'Stop it'!"

Still no ". . ."

"I'm going to . . . and I mean business!"

Now who on earth would believe that? What finally happens is that the child moves on to the next challenge and the parent sighs, "Oh, you're going to be the death of me!"

What you are doing with that routine is producing a tragic credibility gap. It takes more courage to ". . ." than it does to continue to harangue. But if you carry through with the promised punishment, you build the child up and give him security. You can loosen up as he grows older and is able to handle more responsibility and freedom for decision–making. A three- or four-year-old does not have the maturity to make the family policy decisions, as I see some forced to do.

30

Preadolescence

Competition and industry are hallmarks of this time in life. The child is more secure emotionally and is resting before the turmoil of adolescence. He has honed his motor skills and intellectual capacities, and he must try them out on the world. He needs to win approval and self-confidence, most appropriately and critically from his parents.

Living in the minister's home in the age of the suburban church places your sons and daughters in a desirable social and educational setting. Good schools, scouting, and summer camping may be available. These activities provide the arena for the preadolescent to discover and sharpen his skills. Involvement in church programs increases his opportunities to receive encouragement and praise.

These, however, will never substitute for time spent with parents, gaining their unquestioned approval, ingredients which are most susceptible to erosion. You and your wife may be overextended in the duties of the church and community. You may rely on the schools, church, or scouting to meet your children's needs. This can easily happen, because children are reluctant to ask directly for the parental attention they crave. Rather than say, "Dad, I want more of your time," the request comes as a rude and embarrassing demand, such as failing school performance or delinquency.

Kathy is a lovely, bright, and capable teen-ager who recently was arrested on a drug abuse charge. What were the causes of her sudden rebellion? She was described as an independent, self-reliant child. She had caused no concern because she always seemed capable and involved in group activities outside the home.

When I talked with Kathy, I heard a different story. "They never cared what I was doing," she reported. "My brothers were always going places with mother and daddy. I was left out. They never gave me any attention, so I finally just gave up."

You must realize that *every* child wants to spend time with you individually and with the family. He may kick and scream about leaving his friends, but that is soon forgotten and he is reassured that you want him and include him as a vital part of the family.

Gaining attention through disobedience carries the uncertainty of whether daddy is really interested in "me," or simply in what "they" will think of "him." Time spent with your child when everything is going well is far more valuable for his self-esteem.

I can't overemphasize the importance of giving your preadolescent the clear message of self-worth and acceptance. In all probability, by the time you have a child in this age group you have other children. Consequently, each must be recognized as an individual. They are not all alike; their temperaments and abilities may vary drastically. So will your attitude, conscious and unconscious, toward each one. Try to become aware of these feelings and such destructive patterns as scapegoating one child or making unfavorable comparisons.

Keep uppermost in your mind ways to build up your child. Do you put down his ideas and creativity? Get in touch with your reasons for this, and don't load him down with the same unrealistic expectations with which you are burdened. Give him responsibilities he can carry out, and reward his successes.

31

Adolescence

One of my teachers likened adolescence to the awesome moment for an aerialist when he has released his grip on one trapeze and is reaching for the next, perhaps with a somersault or two in between. The teen-ager has left the relative security of childhood and is grasping for adulthood. He is faced with physical changes, sexual maturity, peer pressures, volatile emotions, a great desire for independence, and formidable fears which are only half realized. It is a thrilling time of flying exuberantly there in the big top, but a terrifying moment of wondering if there is a net down below. Adolescence is a time of idealism and commitment, a time of boundless energy and irresponsible laziness.

Since the peer group and parent surrogates achieve unmeasured prominence, now your children can have a great advantage. The church people may provide these abundantly. The adolescent has the opportunity to make his commitment toward a peer group which is Christ-centered. His risk-taking can take the form of a courageous stand for Christian principles. The adult model he chooses may be a committed Christian.

He may even fall back into the safety net of parental limits with little fear of peer rejection. Since his daddy is a preacher, they let him off the hook. In our society of situation ethics, it can be comforting for him to have a stable base to come back to from time to time. At this time, especially, parents should be turned on to listening and understanding, thereby opening the door to effective communications. As counselors you are keenly aware of this principle; just try to put it into practice with your children. Through this avenue such issues as adult hypocrisy, materialism, handling emotions, sexual attitudes and behavior, drug use, and vocational choices may be discussed.

Like the rest of us, adolescents need acceptance, affection, approval, and the security of limits. Life as a p.k. may threaten any one of these areas when you consciously or unconsciously begin to sacrifice your child on the altar of service to the church, or to the expectations of the community. When you are too busy to know him, too distracted to listen, or too self-centered to show interest and give him approval, the sacrifice is made.

Minister First—Father Second?

A highly respected minister of an urban church in the east has had the pain of seeing his son suffer from emotional disturbance, which led to prolonged psychiatric hospitalization. An important factor in the boy's depression and drug abuse had been his feeling of losing his father to the church. The minister was recently debating with himself about accepting an invitation to speak at an important meeting in another city, knowing his family would much prefer that he stay at home. Sad to say, his primary consideration seemed to be the number of important people who would hear him speak if he accepted the invitation, rather than building up the seriously undermined relationships at home.

Dealing with adolescents is often a frightening prospect for parents to consider. Your little boy or girl is suddenly as big as you are and may be seen as a time bomb waiting to go off. If early relationships were not built strongly, and responsibility and respect established, adolescents are just that—time bombs. They are impulsive, extremely sensitive to peer pressure, have wheels, and most frightening of all to most parents, they have sexual drives to cope with.

There are two general guidelines I'd like to share with you. The first is preventive in nature, the second preventive and therapeutic.

Restrict Early—Permit Later

A valuable concept with which to begin childrearing is that of restricting early and increasing permissiveness late. This is so obvious as to be almost laughable. When a child is small, easily controlled, and needs outside restraints, that is the time to restrict. Then it is possible. When he reaches the age of fifteen, it's too late to start a program he has never known. It's too late for the ". . ."!

When the child is reaching maturity he should be prepared to handle more freedom—not complete freedom, but gradually increasing responsibility for self. He should be allowed, and expected, to exercise his internal controls. Those should have been in the making since he was a toddler.

Acceptance and Trust

This brings us to the second principle: acceptance and trust. These may be transmitted in many ways. One way is through the increase in freedoms allowed, and avoiding interrogations with an air of mistrust.

Another is through communication. The most common complaint I hear from adolescents is, "They don't listen to me." The necessary ingredient for communication is listening. That takes practice, for most of us are too busy preparing our rebuttal to listen to the other side. Both parent and child must agree to listen and be sensitive to non-verbal messages.

Acceptance and trust are also transmitted by your taking time for involvement. The message is, "I'm important enough for him to take time for me." We sometimes act as though we think families somehow just "happened" and children raise themselves. Of course, we all know that isn't true. In fact, I think we are sometimes overwhelmed by the responsibility and try to avoid it. Unfortunately, we attempt to justify our avoidance by our involvement in the ministry.

Christ warned that "it is better to be thrown into the sea with a millstone around your neck than to cause one of these little ones to stumble." You must honestly evaluate your performance as fathers. This role, among the many you are asked to fill, is of primary importance. You must find or make time for your children, the one flock for which you are most critically responsible. To do this may take a concerted effort in family life education for your church, with *your* family needs being specified and emphasized as well as those of the other church families.

The man of God is a man with the same needs as other men. This is what I have been trying to say in this book.

Suggested Readings

Part I.

Erik Erikson. *Childhood and Society*. New York: Norton, 1950.

Elizabeth O'Connor, *Eighth Day of Creation*. Waco: Word, Inc. 1971.

Edith Schaeffer. *L'Abri*. Wheaton: Tyndale, 1969.

Wayne E. Oates. *The Psychology of Religion*. Waco: Word, Inc. 1973.

Part II.

Elizabeth O'Connor. *Search for Silence*. Waco: Word, Inc. 1972.

Henri J. M. Nouwen. *The Wounded Healer*. New York: Doubleday, 1972.

William Hulme. *Your Pastor's Problems*. Minneapolis: Augsburg, 1966.

Seward Hiltner. *Ferment in the Ministry*. Nashville: Abingdon, 1969.

Judd, Mills, and Burch. *Ex-Pastors*. Philadelphia: Pilgrim Press, 1970.

Part III.

Elton Trueblood. *The Common Ventures of Life*. Waco: Word Paperback, 1975.

Francis Schaeffer. *The Mark of a Christian*. Downers Grove: Inter-varsity Press, 1970.

Carlyle Marney. *Priests to Each Other*. Valley Forge: Judson Press.

E. B. Bratcher. *Centers for the Ministry*. Interseminary Conference, Feb. 19, 1974, Nashville, Tenn.

Part IV.

James L. Cooper. "Where to Go for Help," *Search*, Vol. 5, No. 4, p. 45, 1975.

Part V.

James A. Knight. *A Psychiatrist Looks at Religion and Health*. Nashville: Abingdon, 1964.

Rollo May. *Man's Search for Himself*. New York: Signet, 1953.

Thomas Harris. *I'm O.K. You're O.K.* New York: Harper and Row, 1969.

Peter Fletcher. *Understanding Your Emotional Problems*. New York: Hart, 1958.

Paul Tournier. *To Understand Each Other*. Atlanta: John Knox, 1967.

Paul Tournier. *The Meaning of Persons*. New York: Harper and Row, 1957.

Karl Meninger. *Whatever Became of Sin*. New York: Hawthorn, 1973.

David Augsburger. *Caring Enough to Confront*. Glendale: Regal, 1974.

C. G. Jung. *Analytical Psychology, Its Theory and Practice*. New York: Pantheon, 1968.

Part VI.

James Mallory. *The Kink and I*. Wheaton: Victor Books, 1975.

Jack Taylor. *One Home Under God*. Nashville: Broadman, 1974.

Dorothy Pentecost. *The Pastor's Wife and the Church*. Chicago: Moody Press, 1964.

Lora Lee Parrott. *How to Be a Preacher's Wife and Like It*. Grand Rapids: Zondervan, 1956.

Ingrid Trobisch. *The Joy of Being a Woman*. New York: Harper Jubilee, 1975.

Page Williams. *Do Yourself a Favor, Love Your Wife*. Plainfield: Logos International, 1973.

Walter Trobisch. *I Married You*. New York: Harper and Row, 1971.

John Howell. *Growing in Oneness*. Convention Press, 1972.

Gladys Hunt. *Focus on Family Life*. Grand Rapids: Baker, 1970.

Part VII.

M. B. Rothenberg, "Effects of Television Violence on Children and Youth" J. A. M. A., Vol. 234, No. 10, p. 1043.

Haim Ginott. *Between Parent and Child*. New York: Macmillan, 1965.

Haim Ginott. *Between Parent and Teenager*. New York: Avon, 1969.

James Dobson. *Hide or Seek*. Old Tappan: Revell, 1974.

Erik Erikson. *Identity, Youth and Crisis*. New York: W. W. Norton, 1968.

John Huffman. *Becoming a Whole Family*. Waco: Word, Inc. 1975.